Gurdjieff and the secrets of Beelzebub

New Edition

Egidio Maria Bruno Presta

Independently Published

Who has no conscience, looks for it in the definitions.

EMB Presta

Introduction

The search for knowledge has never ceased to characterize the lives of men. Since its appearance on Earth, man has always sought answers about himself, the universe, life and death. The split between the various systems of knowledge, such as the apparent irremediable gap between science and religion, clearly demonstrates a fundamental division that resides mainly within man. When different systems of knowledge contradict each other without ever arriving at a conciliation, it means that we have observed from different points of view what we want to know, without being able to grasp their mutual relations. One of the causes that prevents the unfolding of understanding in man is precisely this fragmented knowledge, and since the fragmentation of these systems derives from an internal fragmentation of man, consequently, it is man fragmented within himself that he can never reach a correct knowledge of himself and of the universe. The body, the mind and the feeling constitute three instruments of knowledge and only a full synergy between these different parts can provide man with an exact knowledge of himself and of the universe in which he lives.

The systems of knowledge coming from the whole man are integral in their turn and therefore equivalent to a religious science and a scientific religion. This union must also occur for art, as for all other systems of knowledge: a scientific art, an artistic science, a religious art and an artistic religion. In the face of phenomena such as homosexuality, for example, apparently paradoxical in relation to sex as a function of nature to ensure the continuity of the species, science, religion and politics do not know what to catch. The first considers the question in terms of illness, the second from the point of view of religious morality and the third sees everything in relation to rights. All these theories and points of view never capture the essence of this simple phenomenon, and contribute only to manufacture bricks for the construction of a new tower of Babel. Sex has its raison d'etre in the propagation of the species and in the production of some substances required by Nature.

The appearance of homosexuality indicates a provision taken by Nature, when the total number of human beings exceeds the required threshold in a given place and period. Together with the increase and reduction of births, the raising and lowering of mortality, the appearance or absence of homosexuality is another means available to nature to restore a certain balance that has been lost. Anything that exists is part of nature's plans. In the great world wars, there was an increase in the mortality rate and nature was forced to take action, so every family, despite poverty, gave birth to ten children. Nothing happens according to our will. Everything is the result of the laws and purposes of Nature. The conception of

Nature is forced to take certain measures only because the human being does not fulfill his conscious duties towards it, otherwise these phenomena, as well as wars, would have no reason to occur. The current state of human knowledge systems is well illustrated by the parable of the blind and the elephant.

Beyond Ghor there was a city whose inhabitants were all blind. One day, a king arrived there, accompanied by his court and an entire army and camped in the desert. Now, this monarch possessed a mighty elephant, which he used both in battle and to increase the subjection of people. The people were anxious to know what the elephant was like, and some of the members of the blind community rushed to its discovery. Not knowing the shape or the contours of the elephant, they began to feel it blindly and gather information by touching some of its parts. Each of them thought he knew something about the elephant for having touched a part of it. When they returned to their fellow citizens, they were soon surrounded by greedy groups, all anxious, and wrongly, to know the truth by the mouth of those who were themselves mistaken. They asked questions about the form and appearance of the elephant, and listened to everything that was said about them. When asked about the nature of the elephant, the one who had touched his ear answered: "It is a big thing, rough, wide and long, like a carpet". The one who had touched the trunk said: "I know what it is: it looks like a straight and empty pipe, horrible and destructive". One who had touched a paw said: "It is powerful and stable as a pillar". the one who had touched his ear answered: "It is a big thing, rough, wide and long, like a carpet". The one who had touched the trunk said: "I know what it is: it looks like a straight and empty pipe, horrible and destructive". One who had touched a paw said: "It is powerful and stable as a pillar". the one who had touched his ear answered: "It is a big thing, rough, wide and long, like a carpet". The one who had touched the trunk said: "I know what it is: it looks like a straight and empty pipe, horrible and destructive". One who had touched a paw said: "It is powerful and stable as a pillar".

Each of them had touched one of the many parts of the elephant. Everyone's perception was wrong. No one knew him in his entirety: knowledge does not belong to the blind. Everyone imagined something and the image they had was wrong. Not only is there a split between science, religion, art, and so on, but these divisions manifest themselves within each and every discipline, and all this merely demonstrates in what state of blindness man is.

The other problem concerns the general conviction of retaining the current epoch as the highest point ever reached by the human being in terms of knowledge. In fact, many facts show that various fragments of an ancient knowledge qualitatively superior to the current one have come down to us, but they have always been misunderstood and mixed with a lot of fantasies, until Gurdjieff arrived who presented to the world this know in full and correct: the great knowledge that for a long time had been guarded by some great men.

Chapter 1 - The world upside down

The moment when the difference between a life wholly dominated by automatic psycho-emotional associations and the possibility that the human being can become the creator of his actions, and not react more blindly like an automaton driven by forces, is profoundly understood external from the environment, which makes it in all respects identical to a typewriter, a blender, a TV to which you can change channels by pushing a button, it becomes easier to understand many other things.

First of all, we understand that the division between the "conscious" and the "subconscious" of psychology is disproved by the experimental facts, since man in the ordinary state presents himself as an automaton, a puppet moved by external forces, a living dummy, and in him there is nothing that can really be defined as conscious. The illusion of being conscious comes from the uninterrupted identification with all its fragmented "me" which constitute its artificial personality.

It is easy to understand that a psychology that ignores such a fundamental error can not offer either the means to know each other better, nor the tools for real change, and all of its "art" will consist in trying to make changes to the personality. which constitutes the outer shell of man, in his mask, so that it conforms to the needs of a sick society, whose foundations rest on the exploitation of man over man, violence, beautiful words and slavery. From this perspective, if we now take a look at the world of art, we will understand that among all the ordinary artists there can not be any talent or genius, which are nothing but empty words, profound group hallucinations. Man in the state of automaton can not create anything, in him something is created on the basis of accidental psycho-emotional associations to which he obeys and which are erroneously called "artistic inspirations." An artist can not create anything until he leaves the state of automaton, and everything that happens in him is imitation. Moreover, there is no value even in the virtuosos of the technique, as these virtuosities are nothing more than the refinement of acquired motor automatisms. The difference between sacred art and bacchanal art coincides with the difference between a truly awake man and a deeply asleep man who blindly obeys the automatic motions of internal psycho-emotional associations, provoked by external forces. "An artist can not create anything until he leaves the state of automaton, and everything that happens in him is imitation. Moreover, there is no value even in the virtuosos of the technique, as these virtuosities are nothing more than the refinement of acquired motor automatisms. The difference between sacred art and bacchanal art coincides with the difference between a truly awake man and a deeply asleep man who blindly obeys the automatic motions of internal psycho-emotional associations, provoked by external forces. "An artist can not create anything until he leaves the state of automaton, and everything that happens in him is imitation. Moreover, there is no value even in the virtuosos of the technique, as these virtuosities are nothing more than the refinement of acquired motor automatisms. The difference between sacred art and bacchanal art coincides with the difference between a truly awake man and a deeply asleep man who blindly obeys the automatic motions of internal psycho-emotional associations, provoked by external forces.

Highlighting this fundamental difference, it is even irrelevant to emphasize that the sleeping man uses art for ignoble ends, such as trade, the accompaniment of orgiastic dinners or more generally, to outline his rituals in which others do not it is celebrated that the unconscious abandon oneself to its weaknesses. All the ideas automatically accepted by most people deprived of independent critical thinking, which consider art as a fundamental aspect of education, appear in this perspective, absolutely inconsistent, until the need to bases so that man does not remain an automaton.

The state of conscious man corresponds to the simultaneous and synergistic functioning of the three brains: intellectual, emotional and instinctive / motor. All ordinary art is instead produced by partial men, so much so that we have three types of common art, a purely sexual coming from man in which the functioning of the instinctive / motor brain predominates, the second of an emotional type that manifests itself through the unbalanced man in whom the emotional brain regulates its automatic manifestations, and finally a third type of intellectual matrix. He is completely ignorant of the existence of any kind of art coming from conscious men. For this reason and at present, art should never be evaluated through feeling, as it is completely unconscious in relation to it. The same music can produce opposite effects in two different people, because in one they remember, for example, when he lost love and in the other when he found love. Love itself must be assessed by its degree of consciousness, while there is an abuse of the word love which is used to cover one's weaknesses and meanness and to define a set of phenomena, such as possession, jealousy, violence and sexual pleasure that have nothing to do with love, therefore, even for love, conscience must be the universal yardstick. Considering the fact that understanding results from the parallel development of being and knowledge, it is easy to understand how the division between religion and science is absolutely wrong and inconvenient, as both the one and the others are essential for understanding. If we also rely on the principle that by studying man we study the universe and studying the universe we study man, we realize that all these fragmentations of knowledge can only come from people without understanding, this means that the know that we have available is of an excessively poor quality. However, ordinary science and ordinary religion, as we find them at present, are relatively useful, the first for technological developments that in theory should improve the material life of man, and the second to act as an inner policeman in people unconscious, but neither these two homeless tasks are performed at best. But ... everything here. S '

Not only do fragments between apparently opposing disciplines exist, but within each discipline taken individually, other new fragments appear.

We will not talk about the innumerable absurd fragmentations between different religions, as well as those inside the same fundamental religion.

Let's look at the science for a moment. Have you ever wondered why there is quantum physics, classical physics, and so on?

Is simple. One of the fundamental errors of science is having exchanged the laws of the second, third and fourth order with the fundamental laws of which it does not even suspect its existence. This situation corresponds to having exchanged the effects with the causes. This is the reason why it is so complex. You look at the complexity of science and think about what genius is the human intellect. The truth is precisely the opposite.

These are the many errors that make things more and more complex. With each mistake, complexity increases to the square, and if the error concerns something fundamental, the complexity increases to the cube and even more. The four fundamental interactions of physics are not the basic laws, but simple effects produced by causes that correspond to the fundamental cosmic laws (the laws of 3 and 7) that current science ignores.

The absolute proof that they are not fundamental lies in the fact that each of them has a domain in a certain precise scale, after which they lose consistency. Gravity dominates the world of galaxies, but when it comes to the subatomic world it must pass the baton to the strong nuclear force. These "towers of scientific Babylon" are erected because it is ignored that understanding is dictated by the degree of being. In a man who does not have a developed being, understanding will be miserable. When the human being is fragmented even his knowledge will be fragmented and therefore false. This is the difference between subjective science and true science, the science of the whole. All today's scientific theories to explain the universe are trash.

The other problem of current science is ignorance about a large chunk of unknown materials that make up the universe, and the estimate is about 80%.

80% of the mass is missing which must account for the observed gravitational effects and hence the dark matter hypothesis.

Here, we are in the realm of ultra-subtle subjects, which also affect our psychic life, the subjects that make up our emotional life, the very matter of animal magnetism, and so on. In this realm of unknown subjects there are speeds that far exceed that of light. Those who by ignorance or fashion see in quantum physics who knows what revolution are illusioned. As for esotericism and philosophy, I will be extremely synthetic. Esotericism is a pile of manure in which very few precious pearls are dispersed that only those with a high degree of discernment can identify and thus avoid falling into error, and since with a few pearls you can not make a necklace, you do not it can reach nothing if not through the integral science that ordinary esoterism does not possess.

All the other forms of pseudo-spirituality created by clever people and for commercial purposes are always defined by the wisdom of his grandfather: "Laboratori for the improvement of psychopathy".

Chapter 2 - Gurdjieff and the custodians of great knowledge

In the inner life of Gurdjieff, thanks to a correct education given him by his father and his first teachers, he developed a deep desire to find the answers to various questions that life faced him. What is the purpose and the real nature of the human being? What are the important events that happened in the remote past of our planet and why do ancient and modern historians seem to grope in the dark? Is it possible that during all these millennia, no one among men has ever been able to discover the truth? If someone has managed to discover the truth, why has this great knowledge never been handed down to the present day for the benefit of everyone? Why do wars exist? Why do men fall prey to such madness that leads them to mutual destruction?

To the young eyes of Gurdjieff, everything seemed to make no sense and an unstoppable force developed in him that required him to find these answers to remedy the enormous inner emptiness, typical of those who become aware that the sole satisfaction of animal instincts does not lead to any realization, neither to happiness and indeed, it increases considerably that inner emptiness that no longer leaves any truce to the life of a man. He questioned people who initially seemed to be educated to his young eyes, looked for answers in the scientific disciplines of the period, in psychology, in physics, I went on to study religions and esotericism, but in the end he had to conclude that none of this knowledge provided an answer satisfactory. They were only used as training to foster the development of that discernment, of that flair that for the sincere researcher is like a compass while navigating the boundless sea on a moonless night. He realized definitively that the educated people possessed no real knowledge, that modern science was groping in the darkness like everyone else, and that there was some pearl in religions and esotericism, but it was submerged in a pile of absurdities. However, the existence of these precious pearls from the remotest past clearly demonstrated that the idea of considering our current civilization as the flower blossomed through centuries of slow evolution was utterly wrong, and that this process actually it was done exactly the opposite. There had been no evolution, all the clues showed that the current civilization was the result of a real involution, of a degeneration of some golden age that existed in the past. Not surprisingly, another expression used by Gurdjieff to define his group of researchers, in addition to the one already known as "Truth Seekers", was that of "Seekers of Pearls in Dung". Some of the pearl of great knowledge had survived in spite of the many centuries that had passed, but the eyes had to be made to recognize it in the midst of all that garbage, and all that was not enough, it was not enough to have some fragment to reconstruct integral science. For this reason, all these little pearls scattered among huge heaps of waste called "religions", "esotericism", "occultism", "spirituality", and so on, although useful to make the researcher understand that something really important in the past had been found, they were unusable. Gurdjieff realized that alone, without a real expert guide and with some fragment of the great knowledge in his hands, nothing practical could be achieved and, on the contrary, could prove to be harmful. He understood that the human machine was remarkably complex and any practice without real depth knowledge would have risked compromising mental and physical health. The same degree of difficulty that a bicycle repairer would encounter if he found himself working on the repair of airplanes. Without any doubt, it would do more damage than anything else. He himself learned from an old master that the artificial respiration he was practicing was extremely dangerous, this is because air is one of the three essential nutrients that together with food and impressions enter the human organism in precise proportions, and increase the introduction of one of them without changing the quantity of others inevitably produces imbalances with the consequent damages. . In fact, in those who had practiced artificial respiration without a really expert guidance, and I really mean why many charlatans declared themselves so, there had been damage to the heart. All they had achieved through the practice of artificial respiration was an enlarged heart. Gurdjieff definitively convinced himself that without the guidance of a man who really knows, the results of an arbitrary practice or under the guidance of charlatans, who for their own selfish purposes pretend to be experts, would have been completely opposed to the intended purpose. All these groups, which without real knowledge were used to implement manipulations on the complex human machine, were defined by Gurdjieff "Workshops for the improvement of

Psychopathy", and their followers called them "Candidates for the Fleshroom".

Moreover, each of you if minimally impartial can see for yourself that, nowadays and in most cases with rare exceptions, all those who are interested in spirituality, esotericism, or who say they practice a certain inner discipline, they find themselves in a worse state than that of the common man who lives a certain ordinary life. Gurdjieff, therefore, in the course of his innumerable search for the truth, refined his discernment on various issues. The man who wanted to evolve inwardly, he would have to find an expert guide, roughly as a patient goes to the expert doctor to treat his illnesses.

But had the great knowledge survived to this day? Many facts convinced Gurdjieff that all this was very likely. Among the many events that strengthened this idea in Gurdjieff, there was to see, opening a newspaper by chance, that one of the legends sung by his father was reported on some very old scrolls that archaeologists had found only recently in the course of some excavations. Gurdjieff realized that knowledge, not only had been transmitted verbally over time, but that the owners of the Great Knowledge, these really great men of the past, had made up their minds to find a means of preserving them over the millennia. Art was one of these means used to preserve great knowledge. The Custodes of the Great Knowledge inserted in many works of ancient art all the information of their objective science. Here is what the true art was, the objective art, which exactly like an ark of Noah, had the task of guarding the seeds of the Great Knowledge, so that they would not perish through the universal flood constituted by wars, natural disasters and degeneration the resulting global, in which all the great achievements of the past fall into oblivion and the few surviving fragments are misinterpreted. One of these works of Objective Art is the Sphinx. This event was only one among many that convinced Gurdjieff that somewhere on the planet there must have been men who still possessed this great knowledge. After exhausting research, endless journeys conducted in extreme conditions, in which some of his friends died, Gurdjieff managed to find these men located in a place in Central Asia. A confraternity inaccessible to the rest of the world: the true Keepers of Great Knowledge.

The opera *"The stories of Beelzebub to his nephew"*, written by Gurdjieff in the second half of the twentieth century, is a true masterpiece of Objective Art. In it, Gurdjieff transmits to us a knowledge of the highest qual'ty, different from the poor knowledge that we assimilate through modern culture. This work tells us, in both a literary and an allegorical form, the Great Knowledge. The allegorical part consists of the 3 main characters who travel the entire work and have 7 precise meanings. All the rest of the work makes us part of some important events that happened in the past of our planet, unknown to ancient and modern historians, facts that constitute the same "spiritualizing factor" that had the legends of Gurdjieff's father, teach us the principles of objective science, of objective art, and so on. We learn what events have happened in the past that have led humanity to live such a disastrous life, how the men of the past have discovered the Great Knowledge and how it has been lost due to cataclysms, wars and revolutions, and what were the means used to preserve it for the objective good of future generations. All this high quality knowledge present in Gurdjieff's work constitutes a useful tool for us based on the principle that understanding is the result of the proportional development of knowledge and being, and since these two factors influence each other, it is easy to infer that poor quality knowledge also affects the development of being. For these reasons the first work of Gurdjieff, as he himself declares, *"To eradicate from the thought and the feeling of the reader, ruthlessly and without the slightest compromise, the beliefs and the opinions, rooted for centuries in the psychism of men, concerning all that exists in the world".* If the building consisting of the poor knowledge we have acquired is not destroyed, nothing can be built. For these reasons, Gurdjieff makes us aware of real facts that have occurred in the past, which give us a completely different view from that which has been formed in us through the knowledge of ordinary history, ordinary science, ordinary religions, and so on. . Listening to the narratives of Beelzebub, is tantamount to hearing the same voice of those great men of the past who tell us of the events happening on planet Earth, which explain the laws of objective science, the science of everything, and show us what are our real possibility through the science of being.

Reading *"Beelzebub's tales to his nephew"* is like sitting down today, next to one of those great men of the past who guarded the Great Knowledge and learn by listening to everything told by his own voice. Today, many of the people who have approached this work are lacking the minimum degree of understanding required and already acquired through previous efforts.

In the conviction that they are already able to understand, these scoundrels are spreading, without redness on their faces, in complete unconsciousness, various imaginary interpretations, in which, through their fervid imagination, they conceive of absurdities in an allegorical key.

The greatest disaster is not so much in the fact that these people with a passionate fantasy are already in themselves misguided, but that they are dominated by one of their most frequent and widespread weaknesses, that is to want to appear at all costs wise to the eyes of others, they do a lot of work to educate others in the art of going off the road. After all, nothing new under the sun, is the usual old story that repeats itself in accordance with the laws. For this reason, it is essential that everyone does everything to develop that discernment that, as I always say, is the only and only compass while sailing on the high seas in a moonless night.

Chapter 3 - Gurdjieff's extraordinary historical knowledge

The first extraordinary coincidence in the historical chronicles reported by Gurdjieff, is that between a legend that sang his father and the myth of Atlantis present in Plato's *Timaeus* and *Crizia* . In this legend sung by the father of Gurdjieff, and reported in the book *"Encounters with extraordinary men"*, it tells the story of the great civilization of the island of Haninn that was located where Greece is currently in the period called *"flood before the flood "*, or seventy generations before the last flood, where each generation corresponded to a hundred years. The only men to survive this cataclysm called "flood before the flood" were the members of the Imastun scientific brotherhood, which were scattered throughout the earth with the aim of conducting their studies of astrology, so as to be able to observe the different effects produced by celestial influences on various areas of the planet. After that, the results obtained from their research were communicated using telepathy by means of some pitas that functioned as real receiving antennas.

Other information regarding these historical events seems to be contained also in the book " *The stories of Beelzebub to his nephew*"in the chapter " *Beelzebub professional hypnotist*", when we talk about the sinking of the island Siapura located north of the island of Cyprus due to a planetary earthquake which was also one of the two causes of the desertification of Egypt, once a very luxuriant land.

From these indications we understand that " *seventy generations before the last flood*"are equivalent to seven thousand years before the last flood. If the last flood occured around 3100 BC, as the results of the studies on the studies seem to indicate surveys of sediments in today's Iraq, and which many make to coincide with that narrated by the Mesopotamian poems (Atrahasis, Utnapištim, Ziusudra), the era in question is located about 10,000 BC

If all this is correct, the period indicated by Plato is the same as suggested by Gurdjieff's father, not only, the other amazing coincidence consists in the fact that both, the father of Gurdjieff and Plato, refer to the existence in that period of two great civilizations, that of the Atlanteans and that of the Greeks. The only difference lies in the fact that Plato refers to this era by the sinking of Atlantis, while Gurdjieff places the cataclysm that determined the end of Atlantis much earlier. Here's what Plato reports in *Crizia* :

" *Let me begin by observing, first of all, that at 9,000 the years that have passed since the war are over, as was said, there was among those who lived beyond the Pillars of Hercules and those who lived within them, this war I am going to describe. On the combatants, it is said that on one hand the city of Athens was at the head and that he fought by measuring himself in war, on the other hand the fighters were commanded by the kings of Atlantis who, as I said, was a larger island in extension of Libya and Asia. Before that narrow mouth called the Pillars of Hercules, there was an island. And this island was bigger than Libya and Asia together, and from it you could move to other islands and from these to the mainland in front ...*

In later times ..., having succeeded earthquakes and extraordinary cataclysms, in the turn of a day and a bad night ... all in mass sank under the ground, and the Atlantis island similarly swallowed by the sea disappeared and that, afterwards hit by an earthquake, it became an insurmountable mud barrier for travelers who sailed across the ocean. "

Twenty-nine years ago they report the events narrated at about the same time as indicated by Gurdjieff's father, that is, in 10,000 BC

In Plato's Timaeus, Solon learns from the Egyptian priests the existence of a great Greek civilization of which the Greeks of the time no longer hold any memory and always placed in the period in question, 10,000 BC

The speech made by the Egyptian priest to Solon and reported in Plato's Timaeus is also extremely significant:

" *There is in Egypt",* he began to recount that, *"in the Delta, at whose summit the course of the Nile divides a district called Saiticus, and Sais is the most important city of this district, the city from which King Amasi also came . For the inhabitants a goddess was the founder of the city, and her name in Egyptian is Neith, while in Greek, as they say, Athena: they are very friends of the Athenians and in a sense they say they are still relatives with them. "*

Solon said that when he came to that place he was greeted with great honors by them, and having once asked the priests more prepared around these matters on ancient facts, he discovered that neither himself nor any other Greek was, so to speak, aware of these facts. And then, wanting to push them towards the discourses concerning ancient events, he began to talk about those facts that are supposed to be the oldest, and he told of Foroneus who is said to be the first man, and of Niobe, and after the deluge, of how Deucalion and Pyrrha spent their lives, and made the genealogy of their descendants, and remembering the times he tried to calculate in which years the events of which he spoke had occurred. Then one of the very old priests said:

" *Solon, Solon, you Greeks are always children, and there is no old Greek.*"
And Solon, after listening, asked: *"How? What is this thing you say?"*
" *You are all young",* replied the priest, *"in the souls: in fact in them you do not have any ancient opinion that comes from a primitive tradition or even any teaching that is hoary for the age. And this is the reason. Many are and in*

many ways have happened and will occur the losses of men, the largest by fire and water, for many others other minor reasons. That story that tells of you, that is to say that one day Fetonte, son of the Sun, after having pledged his father's cart, because he was not able to drive him along the road of his father, burned everything that was on the earth , and he himself was killed struck by lightning, is told in the form of myth, but in reality it is the deviation of celestial bodies that revolve around the earth and that determines in long periods of time the destruction, through a large amount of fire , of all that is on earth. Then those who live in the mountains and in high and dry places die more easily than those who live near the rivers and the sea: and the Nile, which saves us in other things, even in that case saves us from that calamity by flooding. "

I will not elaborate on this subject yet, everyone will be able to learn, reading with extreme care the work " *The stories of Beelzebub to his nephew"* of Gurdjieff, what I think is the real history of ancient civilizations. It is told of an Egypt before the sands unknown to historians. Initially Egypt was a thriving land, desertification came only later and was provoked by the same catastrophe that forced the Tikliamuish and Maralpleissis civilizations to move to other more hospitable places, while in the beginning they were located, the first in today's desert of karakum, and the second in the current Gobi desert; all these places were very lush lands. The origin of Sumerian civilization remains unknown to all historians; from Gurdjieff we learn that the Sumerian civilization originated from the Tikliamuish civilization, at a time when the desertification of the Karakum became unstoppable.

Chapter 4 - The union between religion and science

It is necessary to understand, when considering the knowledge possessed by Gurdjieff, that part of it comes from his researches, studies and personal experiments, while the other has been learned by those who have kept it through the millennia up to the present day. . All the concentrations present in the universe, like galaxies, suns, planets, human bodies, atoms, electrons, microbes, are all relative centers because, unlike space, they have a form. The Universe of the galaxies is a single body with a shape that is growing in the infinite space without form, just as the body of a child grows up to become an adult.

All these relative centers originated from the absolute center. The creation of galaxies is, paradoxically, the "Mind of God" that has given itself a body not to die. It is the story of the survival instinct of a creature called God.

Originally, when galaxies and everything else had not yet been created, there existed only the infinite space constituted by eternalkrilno, an inert matter, and the Absolute Sun, an invisible astronomical body that today is the center around which they rotate. all the galaxies and the source from which everything flows and to which everything returns. The Absolute Sun is both the physical brain of God and his mind, and all beings with subtle bodies that inhabit it are the equivalent of neurons in our brains. Man is an almost perfect miniature image of the entire Universe. I used the expression "almost perfect", because in the universe in miniature, that is in us, the action of the Absolute Sun is missing that governs all its parts, in us the real ego is missing, the master who regulates and makes all the harmonic organism. The miniature Universe, that is, Man, will always be a Universe immersed in chaos and without harmony, until he creates the permanent Self, which corresponds to the Absolute Sun of the great Universe. Thus, it can be said that the creation of the human Universe is the inverted and mirror image of the image of the great Universe. In the great Universe it is the Absolute Sun that creates and reigns over everything, in the human universe instead the Absolute Sun, or true I, is created by the parts that already constitute that Universe. Beelzebub tells us about creation, describes why and how the universe was created as we know it. The Absolute Sun, up to that moment, had existed as a creature that obtained nourishment from itself, in fact the two fundamental laws that govern the entire Universe of changing forms, were essentially different. The law that governs the development of processes was based on the principle of continuity of vibrations; the intervals were divided equally, and this law acted only within the Absolute Sun. The Absolute Sun was a self-feeding creature, without the necessity of having to take its nourishment from the outside. With the passage of time, the Absolute Sun, or the "Physical Brain and the Mind of God," realized that it was slow y contracting. The Absolute Sun contracted inexorably, and eventually disappeared into thin air. God, in short, becoming aware of his mortality, realized that he would soon die. they were essentially different. The law that governs the development of processes was based on the principle of continuity of vibrations; the intervals were divided equally, and this law acted only within the Absolute Sun. The Absolute Sun was a self-feeding creature, without the necessity of having to take its nourishment from the outside. With the passage of time, the Absolute Sun, or the "Physical Brain and the Mind of God," realized that it was slowly contracting. The Absolute Sun contracted inexorably, and eventually disappeared into thin air. God, in short, becoming aware of his mortality, realized that he would soon die. they were essentially different. The law that governs the development of processes was based on the principle of continuity of vibrations; the intervals were divided equally, and this law acted only within the Absolute Sun. The Absolute Sun was a self-feeding creature, without the necessity of having to take its nourishment from the outside. With the passage of time, the Absolute Sun, or the "Physical Brain and the Mind of God," realized that it was slowly contracting. The Absolute Sun contracted inexorably, and eventually disappeared into thin air. God, in short, becoming aware of his mortality, realized that he would soon die. the intervals were divided equally, and this law acted only within the Absolute Sun. The Absolute Sun was a self-feeding creature, without the necessity of having to take its nourishment from the outside. With the passage of time, the Absolute Sun, or the "Physical Brain and the Mind of God," realized that it was slowly contracting. The Absolute Sun contracted inexorably, and eventually disappeared into thin air. God, in short, becoming aware of his mortality, realized that he would soon die. the intervals were divided equally, and this law acted only within the Absolute Sun. The Absolute Sun was a self-feeding creature, without the necessity of having to take its nourishment from the outside. With the passage of time, the Absolute Sun, or the "Physical Brain and the Mind of God," realized that it was slowly contracting. The Absolute Sun contracted inexorably, and eventually disappeared into thin air. God, in short, becoming aware of his mortality, realized that he would soon die. he realized he was slowly contracting. The Absolute Sun contracted inexorably, and eventually disappeared into thin air. God, in short, becoming aware of his mortality, realized that he would soon die. he realized he was slowly contracting. The Absolute Sun contracted inexorably, and eventually disappeared into thin air. God, in short, becoming aware of his mortality, realized that he would soon die.

His survival instinct prompted him to find a solution. He had to find a way to be able to supply material from outside, to find the nourishment from the outside useful to prevent the contraction of the mass of the Absolute Sun.

Outside, however, there was only the eternalkrilno, an inert material and therefore unusable for nourishment. He had to find a way to convert eternalkrilno into a material that could become nourishment. In a picturesque way, we could say that God was looking for food and once he found it, he realized that now he should also discover how to cook it in order to make this food eatable and nutritious.

As we shall see, man too will have to transform his nourishment to crystallize those substances which will enable him to attain immortality. It was thus that the Absolute Sun modified the functioning of the two fundamental laws and emanated them outside of itself, the famous Logos, or Word of God. The emanation of the Absolute Sun began to convert the eternal

Kalithno, this inert matter, initially to create the devices that would work as processors of substances. These transformers are the galaxies, the Suns, the planets, the organic life, the man, and so on. Through these transformers the nourishment necessary to avoid dying could have reached the Absolute Sun. God, creating the megalocosm, found the secret to become immortal, and defeated death; if now man creates within himself the Absolute Sun, the unique and real Ego, will have also conquered immortality, otherwise after the death of the physical body, it will vanish into nothingness. Man is somehow in the same situation as the Absolute Sun before creation. In the Universe we have two scales, one that descends from the Absolute Sun, also called creative, involutive, and the other that from below, through various steps, returns to the Absolute Sun, bringing the nourishment necessary to make it live, and is called evolutionary.

The possibility that God has given man to be able to form subtle bodies within himself, therefore the possibility of conquering immortality, is due to the fact that the Absolute Sun in addition to the need to receive nourishment in order to survive, also has a other necessity. This last necessity consists in this: since the creation process began, the body of the created Universe, so to speak, is continuously growing. The process of creation is not something that has happened once and is now over; if it were to end, God would again come to terms with that famous problem of contraction that would lead him to death. The process of creation is perpetual, the body of the Universe grows and expands, and together with it the Absolute Sun is also expanding; if the body grows, the brain also grows, and a growing brain needs other neurons, which would be individuals provided with the subtle body, or body of the soul, a body made up of suitable materials for living on the Absolute Sun. Here, the reason why we humans have been given the possibility of being able to form within us subtle bodies and therefore become immortal and survive death. But mind you, it's just a possibility. It is necessary to understand that a life conducted in the usual ordinary and automatic way does not allow the luxury of forming a soul and the destiny that awaits the human being who lives only immersed in the pleasures of the flesh is eternal extinction. It fades into nothingness. The idea that man already has a soul is just a story told to make children fall asleep when the evening comes. In other words, if someone wants absolute extinction after the death of the physical body, he does not have to do anything, he can simply continue to live in an ordinary way. If instead eternal death does not go down, then it must work to do what must be done, knowing that what can be done now will no longer be tomorrow. Time is pressing and eternal death is coming inexorably, but to achieve this it is essential to sacrifice many things. Nothing can be achieved without voluntary and conscious sacrifices, without conscious work and voluntary suffering. knowing that what can be done now will no longer be tomorrow. Time is pressing and eternal death is coming inexorably, but to achieve this it is essential to sacrifice many things. Nothing can be achieved without voluntary and conscious sacrifices, without conscious work and voluntary suffering. knowing that what can be done now will no longer be tomorrow. Time is pressing and eternal death is coming inexorably, but to achieve this it is essential to sacrifice many things. Nothing can be achieved without voluntary and conscious sacrifices, without conscious work and voluntary suffering.

Modern science, ordinary philosophy, the state religions, the various forms of spirituality, esotericism, can not provide any practical help, both for the purposes mentioned above, and to help the understanding of the true essence of this universe and of our life. Only a people of warmongers like the Terrans could conceive the Big Bang Theory, which sees the beginning of the universe as if it were a bomb attack; and always and only a belligerent people could have in its uses and customs the habit of celebrating by exploding fireworks.

In every action of man, even in what he erroneously defines with the high-sounding name of "love", violence is omnipresent. Modern science ignores the two fundamental laws, which is equivalent to ignoring the causes. It continually exchanges effects due to causes. The four fundamental forces of physics, ie gravitational interaction, electromagnetic interaction, weak nuclear interaction and strong nuclear interaction, are not fundamental cosmic laws. The proof of this lies in the fact that the domain that has each of these interactions is limited to a precise scale, after which their strength loses consistency.

The gravitational force is valid in the world of galaxies, in the subatomic world it loses its dominion, and the strong nuclear interaction comes into play, which after all is only a hypothesis, nothing proved, it is only an arbitrary explanation to make go back to the accounts, to be able to explain how they do the protons that make up the nucleus of the atom not to repel and then to undermine the atom since they are all of positive charge and should repel. Then, they think: "Certainly there exists, in the subatomic scale, a force that is more intense than the electromagnetic force, by which the repulsion between the protons is neutralized, and since it is so strong, we will call it: force or strong nuclear interaction, and so on. "So this is subjective science, after all.

As demonstrated, therefore, it is impossible to explain the Universe through second-order, third-order laws, it is tantamount to confusing the effects with the causes. For this reason all scientific theories are fundamentally incorrect. If science knew the two laws of the first order, the two fundamental and cosmic laws, which act indifferently on all scales, from the microcosm to the macrocosm, would be quite another thing.

If science did not ignore all those subtle materials that today make up about 80% of the missing mass, and that gave rise to the hypothesis of dark matter, it would be another matter. In the list of these unknown subjects would appear those that constitute our emotional, psychic life, etc. We would find that there are speeds that far exceed that of light. If science knew the okidanokh it would understand why protons do not repel. If science knew the okidanokh would understand the true nature of electromagnetic phenomena and would know that the difference in electrical potential, also called voltage, whose unit of measurement is the Volt, is determined by one of the characteristics of the material called okidanokh, or the tendency of this matter, composed of the three sacred forces, to unite in everything. It would also understand, with wonder, the great meaning it has, both this property of the ukidanokh, and the okidanokh itself. Many things would be explained. To really understand the Universe it is necessary to consider it as a living organism that forms a unity made up of multiple organs occupying a well-defined place, which have well-defined functions and mutually support each other on the basis of precise relationships governed by two fundamental laws. The same two fundamental laws which have produced and govern multiplicity, will show us unity, or in what way is united what has been divided. To really understand the Universe it is necessary to consider it as a living organism that forms a unity made up of multiple organs occupying a well-defined place, which have well-defined functions and mutually support each other on the basis of precise relationships governed by two fundamental laws. The same two fundamental laws which have produced and govern multiplicity, will show us unity, or in what way is united what has been divided. To really understand the Universe it is necessary to consider it as a living organism that forms a unity made up of multiple organs occupying a well-defined place, which have well-defined functions and mutually support each other on the basis of precise relationships governed by two fundamental laws. The same two fundamental laws which have produced and govern multiplicity, will show us unity, or in what way is united what has been divided.

The first law demonstrates that all the existing phenomena and on any scale, from the subatomic world to the world of galaxies, are the result of the meeting of three opposing forces.

Without the meeting of three forces, no phenomenon can be produced. It is easy to understand that a force alone can not exist, since to every force there always corresponds a second opposing force of resistance. This means that there can not be energy without matter or vice versa without energy. The other implication is that matter and energy are basically the same identical thing, or to be more precise, two aspects of a single and inseparable phenomenon. The equivalence between matter and energy also demonstrates the impossibility in the Universe of a state of absolute emptiness, that is, a state of absolute absence of matter, and therefore everything takes place in Nature necessarily by transmission. This last principle makes us understand that it is essential to discover all those subtle matters unknown to science, if we really want to know the universe. The infinite space, which is generally considered empty, is therefore constituted by an absolutely subtler and present material in the whole universe.

Astronomer Bruce H. Margon states: *"It is a very embarrassing situation to have to admit that we can not find 80% of the matter in the Universe."*

Hence the hypothesis on dark matter elaborated by today's science, which paradoxically turns out not to be directly observable, but must necessarily exist to account for the observed gravitational effects and to explain the formation and integrity of the galaxies, which otherwise would not have could in no way exist. The difficulties that prevent its detection derive from the fact that it does not emit any electromagnetic radiation and all the instruments that cover the whole spectrum, from radio waves to gamma rays, are perfectly useless. It is easy to understand that we are in the realm of all those subtle substances that go beyond the classic "eye of science." In this new realm of matter there are speeds that exceed innumerable times that of light.

Space is shown to be infinite, since any boundary would imply a separation between two spaces, and the second, if confined in turn, would involve a separation with a third space, and so on to infinity. Just as there can not be a force alone, so a boundary can not exist without two spaces, and so on to infinity.

In other words, even by conceiving a finite space, we would obtain infinity. Even giving shape to space, we would inevitably get the formless. Infinite and formless space absolutely abolish the temporal factor, which means that only the formless has no origin and therefore no end. This is equivalent to timelessness and not to eternity, which in any case remains a temporal factor, and although it may exclude the end, does not necessarily imply the exclusion of a beginning. For example, something could have an origin and exist through endless mutations forever, therefore without an end. Both of these states are present in the Universe.

All this shows that the equivalence between space and time is fundamentally wrong. Let's get closer to the center of gravity of our speech. It is therefore shown that only one force can not exist. Current science considers it possible that two forces alone can produce a phenomenon, but in reality this is impossible. If we consider the principle of leverage, we realize that it can not exist without the intervention of 3 forces and that, although science conceives its functioning, after all it is able to discern two forces: the active and the passive force. In reality, with only two forces we would have no leverage, with the introduction, instead, of the third force, called the conciliation force, which in this case consists of the fulcrum, we have the lever phenomenon. It must be noted, however, that when the lever acts, the third force is also found in the points of force application. The other important thing to note, which also confirms the existence of the third force, is that by moving the fulcrum towards the resistance force, the active force required to lift the weight decreases. The approach of the third force, or force of conciliation, adding to the force of resistance or passive force decreases the demand for active force or power force. This shows that the mutual relatiors between three forces that determine a phenomenon are interdependent. the active force required to lift the weight decreases. The approach of the third force, or force of conciliation, adding to the force of resistance or passive force decreases the demand for active force or power force. This shows that the mutual relations between three forces that determine a phenomenon are interdependent. the active force required to lift the weight decreases. The approach of the third force, or force of conciliation, adding to the force of resistance or passive force decreases the demand for active force or power force. This shows that the mutual relations between three forces that determine a phenomenon are interdependent.

Another important feature of the law of the three forces is that forces can swap places. Having two materials of different densities, at their meeting, the less dense one will behave as active force, while the one with greater density as passive force, but if the matter, which in the first case was less dense and therefore manifested as a conductor of the active force , is found to meet a matter with a density lower than it, as a conductor of the active force will become conductor of the passive force. All three forces can exchange places based on the nature of the phenomena. A matter contains, therefore, all three forces, otherwise it could not even exist, since we said that without the intervention of 3 forces we have no phenomenon, however, on the basis of the different density materials it encounters, it manifests itself as an active, passive or neutralizing force. The law of the three forces is a law valid everywhere, in physics, as in chemistry, in psychology, in the subatomic world as in the world of galaxies. For this reason it is called universal and fundamental. If we study phenomena through only two forces, we will never be able to understand its essence, we will never be able to observe the real world. Ancient science was much more advanced than modern science, as it understood the necessity of the three forces and transmitted this knowledge to posterity through religious teachings. The Christian trinity and Hindu trinity express this lost and misunderstood knowledge. True science and true religion are closely connected, they are not opposed to each other as it happens today between modern science and the Christian religion, and this happens because one is not true science and the other is not true religion, they are both fictitious. The law of the three allows the appearance of the phenomena, after which the processes involving the phenomena are regulated by the second fundamental law. The second fundamental law was also part of ancient science and has been handed down to this day by various means. One of these is music, another is the division of the week in 7 days, etc. The second fundamental law is the same universal and mathematical law that regulates the relationships between the frequencies in the pitch system known as the natural scale. Exactly like the law of the 3 forces, this law also manifests itself in all the scales of the universe, and all processes that take place between phenomena one is not true science and the other is not true religion, they are both fictitious. The law of the three allows the appearance of the phenomena, after which the processes involving the phenomena are regulated by the second fundamental law. The second fundamental law was also part of ancient science and has been handed down to this day by various means. One of these is music, another is the division of the week in 7 days, etc. The second fundamental law is the same universal and mathematical law that regulates the relationships between the frequencies in the pitch system known as the natural scale. Exactly like the law of the 3 forces, this law also manifests itself ir all the scales of the universe, and all processes that take place between phenomena one is not true science and the other is not true religion, they are both fictitious. The law of the three allows the appearance of the phenomena, after which the processes involving the phenomena are regulated by the second fundamental law. The second fundamental law was also part of ancient science and has been handed down to this day by various means. One of these is music, another is the division of the week in 7 days, etc. The second fundamental law is the same universal and mathematical law that regulates the relationships between the frequencies in the pitch system known as the natural scale. Exactly like the law of the 3 forces, this law also manifests itself in all the scales of the universe, and all processes that take place between phenomena The law of the three allows the appearance of the phenomena, after which the processes involving the phenomena are regulated by the second fundamental law. The second fundamental law was also part of ancient science and has been handed down to this day by various means. One of these is music, another is the division of the week in 7 days, etc. The second fundamental law is the same universal and mathematical law that regulates the relationships between the frequencies in the pitch system known as the natural scale. Exactly like the law of the 3 forces, this law also manifests itself in all the scales of the universe, and all processes that take place between phenomena The law of the three allows the appearance of the phenomena, after which the processes involving the phenomena are regulated by the second fundamental law. The second fundamental law was also part of ancient science and has been handed down to this day by various means. One of these is music, another is the division of the week in 7 days, etc. The second fundamental law is the same universal and mathematical law that regulates the relationships between the frequencies in the pitch system known as the natural scale. Exactly like the law of the 3 forces, this law also manifests itself in all the scales of the universe, and all processes that take place between phenomena The second fundamental law was also part of ancient science and has been handed down to this day by various means. One of these is music, another is the division of the week in 7 days, etc. The second fundamental law is the same universal and mathematical law that regulates the relationships between the frequencies in the pitch system known as the natural scale. Exactly like the law of the 3 forces, this law also manifests itself in all the scales of the universe, and all processes that take place between phenomena The second fundamental law was also part of ancient science and has been handed down to this day by various means. One of these is music, another is the division of the week in 7 days, etc. The second fundamental law is the same universal and mathematical law that regulates the relationships between the frequencies in the pitch system known as the natural scale. Exactly like the law of the 3 forces, this law also manifests itself in all the scales of the universe, and all processes that take place between phenomena The second fundamental law is the same universal and mathematical law that regulates the relationships between the frequencies in the pitch system known as the natural scale. Exactly like the law of the 3 forces, this law also manifests itself in all the scales of the universe, and all processes that take place between phenomena The second fundamental law is the same universal and mathematical law that regulates the relationships between the frequencies in the pitch system known as the natural scale. Exactly like the law of the 3 forces, this law also manifests itself in all the scales of the universe, and all processes that take place between phenomena

they are regulated through this law. This law is based on the principle of the discontinuity of vibrations, while current science is convinced of continuity, that is, given an initial force, it proceeds uniformly until the opposing force of resistance runs out. If the concept of physics were correct, we would have found straight lines in nature, which does not happen. The law of the octave manifests itself everywhere, in electromagnetic vibrations, in chemistry, in psychology, and so on. Mathematically it is expressed with the following ratios:

1: 1 - 9: 8 - 5: 4 - 4: 3 - 3: 2 - 5: 3 - 15: 8 - 2: 1

On the other hand, the equal temperament, that is the subdivision of the octave in equal parts, which has almost universally replaced the natural intonation, for reasons of comfort when tonal changes are made, demonstrates all the ignorance of the musical theorists regarding the laws of musical harmony and the laws that govern the entire Universe.

Equivalent temperament corresponds to the same erroneous concept of continuity of vibrations present in physics.

The subdivision of the octave into equal parts, as we shall see, is valid only before the birth of the universe as we know it.

The natural intonation, instead, which divides the octave into unequal parts is the diagram of a law present in nature. Based on these mathematical ratios, we obtain two slowdowns in the progression of the vibrations, the first in the interval between 5: 4 and 4: 3 and the second in the interval between 15: 8 and 2: 1. The implication of these slowdowns is that any process that exists in nature can not proceed if there is no extra external force intervening at the point that constitutes the interval, ie a lateral octave that supports progression and helps it to continue.

If this does not happen, the process is interrupted or the progression 's diverted, until it returns to the starting point by means of continuous deviations. If these intervals did not exist there would be no way to connect the various phenomena of the universe. Through this law, we can understand the precise relationship that exists between the various processes in the universe, interdependence, the place that occupies everything, in other words, the harmony that governs the entire cosmos.

Another property of this law is the development of other octaves from a fundamental sound. Each note of an octave corresponds to an entire octave on an upper plane. In other words, a vibration obtained in a given matter develops an entire octave of vibrations in the less dense matter, and so on, up to a certain specific degree.

The natural harmonics do not correspond to the inner octaves because the development that takes place in them is considered in the same medium of oscillation and propagation, in our case the mixture of air.

Thus, the understanding of musical harmonics is incomplete if it is not known that the development of vibrations can take place even in subtler substances than the air mixture. Subtle materials that penetrate the air and that science ignores.

All objective music, which is able to produce precise results both physical and psychological, is based on the inner octaves.

When the Bukharian dervish Hadji-Assvatz-Truv distinguishes the "creative vibrations" from the "vibrations of inertia", he is referring precisely to this discourse; it is the distinction between acoustic and harmonic vibrations that occur only in the air mixture, and the vibrations that, on the contrary, are able to occur even in the finest materials that penetrate the air; the latter are the only ones that can give concrete results in experiments of objective music, and it is possible to obtain them, as the dervish says, or with goat gut strings or with cords made of a particular metal whose nature is not specified. It is essential to reflect deeply on the particular properties of the fifth stopinder of the sacred heptaparaparshinokh, described in the work "The stories of Beelzebub to his nephew". Who read "

Chapter 5 - The secrets of the law of sects

It is necessary to understand some things about the law of the seven or law of the octave and the law of the three. The law of the octave is the second fundamental cosmic law. It generates, regulates, interconnects and determines the place of all processes in any scale, however, before having processes it is necessary to obtain phenomena. All phenomena take place by means of the law of the three, which is therefore considered as the first fundamental cosmic law. The law of the three shows that any phenomenon can only be produced if the meeting of three forces takes place: one active, one passive and one of conciliation. Current science ignores the existence of this third force. Chemistry ignores that a catalyst is the third force. Mechanics know nothing about the lever principle, the fulcrum constitutes the third force, and that without the third force there can be no lever. The very existence of a matter, an atom or a molecule is due to the meeting of three forces. (see "okidanokh"). For this reason, every matter already contains all three forces within itself, however, only one is manifested on the basis of the events that occur. If a matter of a given density meets a matter of lower density, the former will be conductive of passive force or, in other words, it will manifest itself as a passive force, the latter less dense as an active force, and if the latter encounters a matter with an even lower density, as active, will manifest itself as passive. The third force, whose existence is always ignored, can be found in the result, in the environment or at the point of application. When food arrives in our stomach meets gastric juices, the meeting produces a transformation of food, in this case the third force is found in this resulting result. An example that shows the third force found in the environment is the uterus (environment), when an ovule (passive force) is fertilized by a spermatozoon (active force). If there were no uterus as environment (third force), the only two forces taken into consideration would not be able to produce any phenomenon. Several examples, however, to see the third force at the point of application, we find them in mechanics. It is good, therefore, to keep in mind that a force alone can not exist and that only two forces can never produce any phenomenon. These two laws are called cosmic and fundamental. Cosmic and fundamental are two inseparable properties; if something is cosmic, it is at the same time fundamental, and vice versa. Cosmic means that its dominion and its manifestations extend from the infinitely large to the infinitely small, from the worlds of galaxies to the subatomic worlds. A law with such an extension, to the point of understanding everything, shows us that it comes from the world of causes, from the world from which everything originated, that is from the absolute, for this reason it is also called

Fundamental. from the worlds of galaxies to the subatomic worlds. A law with such an extension, to the point of understanding everything, shows us that it comes from the world of causes, from the world from which everything originated, that is from the absolute, for this reason it is also called Fundamental. from the worlds of galaxies to the subatomic worlds. A law with such an extension, to the point of understanding everything, shows us that it comes from the world of causes, from the world from which everything originated, that is from the absolute, for this reason it is also called Fundamental.

This means that it is a law of the first order, the primary cause from which all other effects arise, ie all other second-order, third-order, fourth-order laws, and so on. The law of universal gravitation, electromagnetic interaction, hypothetical strong nuclear interaction and weak nuclear interaction, all four interactions that current science or subjective science erroneously consider as fundamental, are second, third, fourth and fifth laws order. On a large scale, in the worlds of galaxies, stars, and planets, gravity dominates, after which, having arrived at the world of atoms, its force becomes irrelevant and must give way to electromagnetic interaction, which in turn must yield the place to ' strong nuclear interaction the moment we enter the much smaller scale of atomic nuclei. This shows that we are dealing with secondary laws, tertiary laws, and so on, that is, laws that are effects whose causes lie in fundamental laws. You can not understand the universe by studying the effects regardless of the real causes. It would be like studying an elephant knowing only its proboscis. Confusing effects with causes is one of the most frequent errors of current science. The law of the seven, or law of the octave, has many aspects that must be understood. The universe is a living organism, just like our body. In the universe we have countless materials that vibrate. Where there is matter, we find that it is always in vibration, in it an energy is present, and vice versa, where there is energy, in any case there is matter. The implication is that even the thoughts and emotions are material, and therefore can be weighed and measured. The fact that science can not perform these measurements is because it ignores much of the existing matter in the universe. The so-called "missing mass" of the physical, from which originatec the idea of dark matter.

Rocks, water, air, thoughts anc emotions are all composed of vibrating atoms. To say that in the universe everything is matter, or to say that everything is energy, is equivalent to saying the same thing; in fact it would be more precise to declare that in the universe everything is matter in vibration. In other words, matter and energy are inseparable, they are two aspects of one and the same inseparable phenomenon. The density of each material is inversely proportional to the frequency of vibrations.

The number of vibrations (frequency) of the water atoms is greater if it is in the gaseous state, they decrease if we bring it to the liquid state and continue to decrease if the water is brought to the solid state. Due to the increase in water density, the number of vibrations or frequencies decreases.

The vibration present in matter is a consequence of the vibrations that are produced in it by subtler materials

they penetrate it.

As matter acquires greater density, we have an increase in the strength of resistance that is opposed to the active force of the vibrations produced by a subtler matter. The density of a matter is inversely proportional to its extension in the universe. Less dense is a matter more it is diffused in the universe. The subtlest material in the universe must necessarily have the greatest extension. The more a matter is dense the more it is confined within a given space. It is not by chance that hydrogen which is considered as the least dense element is also the most widespread element in the universe. However, there are innumerable times less dense hydrogen substances which consequently have a much higher diffusion. Matter acquires more density because of its removal from the original source of these vibrations. In seeing that matter is in vibration, we realize that this is an effect, and because behind every effect there is always a cause, it is easy to understand that there must be a point of origin from which these vibrations were produced. This point of origin, being the cause of the effects that we observe, must necessarily be characterized by a force of greater impulse, by a greater number of vibrations which diminish by reason of the removal from it. If we throw a stone, the impulse force is exhausted as it moves away from the origin. This means that a denser material has fewer vibrations, and therefore it is farthest from the original source which produces this impulse force. The matter of a rock is denser than the material that constitutes the mixture of air in which we are immersed, so the rocky matter has a frequency of vibrations lower than that of air. Everything in the universe is alive and provided with intelligence, even rocks. The more dense a subject is, the higher its degree of intelligence is low, and vice versa. This means that in the universe we have different degrees of intelligence and that the origin from which all movements take shape must be more intelligent than anything else existing. That said, it is easy to understand how the Sun of our solar system is the most intelligent being, and that a galaxy has an even higher degree of intelligence, until you get to the center where all the galaxies revolve around, and that will be the highest degree of intelligence in the entire universe. We can call it God, as long as we conceive it as a real astronomical body invisible to us and around which all the galaxies of the universe revolve. This astronomical body is, at the same time, the physical brain and the mind of God. In the whole universe, all these materials in vibration and of different densities evolve and involute continuously. Imagine two "escalators" that move in opposite directions; the first goes downhill, and is the one in which the materials coming from the top undergo the involution, acquiring more density; the second "escalator", the evolutionary one, proceeds in the opposite direction and leads the materials upwards which lose density, they acquire a greater number of vibrations. These vibrating materials can not be changed or evolved without the help of "substance-processing machines". Every concentration existing in the universe, a galaxy, a star, a planet, a plant, an animal, a human being, a molecule, an atom, a microbe, etc., is a machine that has the function of transforming a certain number of substances, both in an evolutionary and in an involutive sense. In turn, all these concentrations or factories for the transformation of the substances themselves undergo a process of involution or evolution. Imagine the universe as a huge factory where all galaxies, suns, planets and humans are machines specialized in the transformation of certain substances. These vibrating materials can not be changed or evolved without the help of "substance-processing machines". Every concentration existing in the universe, a galaxy, a star, a planet, a plant, an animal, a human being, a molecule, an atom, a microbe, etc., is a machine that has the function of transforming a certain number of substances, both in an evolutionary and in an involutive sense. In turn, all these concentrations or factories for the transformation of the substances themselves undergo a process of involution or evolution. Imagine the universe as a huge factory where all galaxies, suns, planets and humans are machines specialized in the transformation of certain substances. These vibrating materials can not be changed or evolved without the help of "substance-processing machines". Every concentration existing in the universe, a galaxy, a star, a planet, a plant, an animal, a human being, a molecule, an atom, a microbe, etc., is a machine that has the function of transforming a certain number of substances, both in an evolutionary and in an involutive sense. In turn, all these concentrations or factories for the transformation of the substances themselves undergo a process of involution or evolution. Imagine the universe as a huge factory where all galaxies, suns, planets and humans are machines specialized in the transformation of certain substances. help with "substance-processing machines". Every concentration existing in the universe, a galaxy, a star, a planet, a plant, an animal, a human being, a molecule, an atom, a microbe, etc., is a machine that has the function of transforming a certain number of substances, both in an evolutionary and in an involutive sense. In turn, all these concentrations or factories for the transformation of the substances themselves undergo a process of involution or evolution. Imagine the universe as a huge factory where all galaxies, suns, planets and humans are machines specialized in the transformation of certain substances. help with "substance-processing machines". Every concentration existing in the universe, a galaxy, a star, a planet, a plant, an animal, a human being, a molecule, an atom, a microbe, etc., is a machine that has the function of transforming a certain number of substances, both in an evolutionary and in an involutive sense. In turn, all these concentrations or factories for the transformation of the substances themselves undergo a process of involution or evolution. Imagine the universe as a huge factory where all galaxies, suns, planets and humans are machines specialized in the transformation of certain substances. a microbe, etc., is a machine that has the function of transforming a certain number of substances, both in an evolutionary and in an involutive sense. In turn, all these concentrations or factories for the transformation of the substances themselves undergo a process of involution or evolution. Imagine the universe as a huge factory where all galaxies, suns, planets and humans are machines specialized in the transformation of certain substances. a microbe, etc., is a machine that has the function of transforming a certain number of substances, both in an evolutionary and in an involutive sense. In turn, all these concentrations or factories for the transformation of the substances themselves undergo a process of involution or evolution. Imagine the universe as a huge factory where all galaxies, suns, planets and humans are machines specialized in the transformation of certain substances.

A star can transform a certain type of substance, while for other substances it is necessary to have a machine like a human being, or a microbe. In the plant world, for example, there are three categories of plants, which correspond to three different machines for the transformation of specific substances. These three categories are generated by the law of the three and are its manifestation. The first category of these plants is made up of machines specialized in transforming only the complex of substances produced by the planet Earth. The second category of plants is used to transform both the set of substances that originate on the planet Earth and those coming from the other planets of the solar system and from the Sun itself. The third and final category of plants, it consists of machines that can transform even the finest substances coming from the worlds of galaxies. The third category of machines includes all those plants containing alkaloids and very thin materials that produce very marked effects on humans, such as coffee, tobacco, opium, hemp, etc. We ourselves are machines that transform various substances. The food we introduce undergoes remarkable transformations, as well as the air we breathe.

The materials that enter these machines undergo various processes of transformation both in an evolutionary and in an involutive way. Thus, there are three types of use of these transformed substances. The first type of processed substances remain in the machine and are indispensable for the further operation of the machine itself. The second and third types of substances, both involutive (waste) and evolutionary, are expelled from the machine that is not specialized for further processing and transferred to other machines that will in turn continue the process of transformation. In this way, the nourishment and mutual support of all that exists exists. All these involutive and evolutionary processes of material transformation are determined, regulated and interconnected by the law of the seven.

$$1/1 - 9/8 - 5/4 - 4/3 - 3/2 - 5/3 - 18/5 - 2/1$$

They are the same fundamental mathematical ratios that the musical theory uses to obtain the natural intonation of the harmonic sounds that go to make up the natural scale. Readers who are not familiar with these principles of objective science will think that we are try'ng to explain the processes that occur between all the phenomena in the universe using music in a bizarre way. For this reason, it is essential to understand immediately that it is precisely the opposite. It is the law of the octave, a law that regulates all the processes existing in the entire universe, to be used to create harmonic relationships in the field of music, that is, in the world of acoustic vibrations. This is because, as we have already explained, the law of the seven is a fundamental cosmic mathematical law that regulates all the vibrational processes of the matter present in the universe, and it is always by means of this law that, once applied to the music, that is to another type of vibratory processes, the acoustic ones , we can get those harmonic sounds that characterize music. The odd thing, rather, is that all the so-called "expert" musicians, as well as all music listeners, ignore that the foundations of music are entirely based on precise mathematical relationships, which are nothing more than the formula of a law that governs all the processes existing in the universe. Pythagoras certainly did not ignore all this when he spoke of the harmony of the spheres, or the "music" of the celestial bodies. In order not to create confusion, for the moment we will leave out the question concerning the ignorance of those musical theorists who, to facilitate tonal changes, have elaborated the tuning system called equal temperament. Now let's try to go into the details of this fundamental cosmic law that was applied after the music. To do this, we can use the music itself. I will use a simpler language as possible, since this article is addressed above all to those who generally find it difficult to understand this law. Mathematical relationships that express this law, namely: Now let's try to go into the details of this fundamental cosmic law that was applied after the music. To do this, we can use the music itself. I will use a simpler language as possible, since this article is addressed above all to those who generally find it difficult to understand this law. Mathematical relationships that express this law, namely: Now let's try to go into the details of this fundamental cosmic law that was applied after the music. To do this, we can use the music itself. I will use a simpler language as possible, since this article is addressed above all to those who generally find it difficult to understand this law. Mathematical relationships that express this law, namely:

1/1 - 9/8 - 5/4 - 4/3 - 3/2 - 5/3 - 18/5 - 2/1

correspond, in the musical sphere, to the notes

Do - Re - Mi - Fa - Sol - La - Yes - Do

But what do these relationships actually express? In music, they express how many times a string of any instrument vibrates at the passing of a second, and how many times the elastic medium vibrates, that is the air, in which this vibratory movement is transferred. The first ratio 1/1 (C) is equal to 1 (one divided one makes one), in other words, the string vibrates only once every second, and so also the vibrations produced in the air will have the same number of vibrations. 9/8 (Re) will be equal to 1,125 vibrations per second (Nine divided eight times 1,125); 5/4 (Mi) at 1.25 vibrations per second; 4/3 (Fa) to 1.33 ... vibrations per second; 3/2 (Sol) to 1.5 vibrations per second; 5/3 (La) at 1.66 ... vibrations per second; 15/8 (Yes) to 1,875 vibrations per second; and finally 2/1 (C) which corresponds to 2, that is, twice the frequency of the first ratio 1/1 (C). As you have observed,

Then, proceeding from the first Do (1/1) to the second Do (2/1) we obtain a gradual increase of the frequency, that is the number of vibrations. By halving the length of a string and maintaining the same tension, we obtain a doubling of the frequency. This phenomenon is almost analogous to the discourse we made at the beginning when they said that by decreasing the density of any matter in the universe there is an increase in the number of vibrations. Another way to increase the frequency of a string is to increase its tension, which is roughly equivalent to decreasing its density and therefore increasing the number of vibrations. The principles that you can observe through music happen in the same way throughout the entire universe. What we said ' now it is only a premise to familiarize yourself with this topic, now we will talk about the law of the eighth or the law of the seven. The whole octave, that is the succession of notes Do - Re - Mi - Fa - Sol - La - Si - Do, in relation to the transformations that the materials present in the universe undergo, clearly shows us how these transformations proceed. Now you have to consider each musical note as a point that indicates the exact situation of any process in progress. Let us again take as an example the process of transformation which all substances present in the universe undergo. Examining all the points of the octave, that is all the notes, we will observe how the process we are considering evolves. The whole octave, that is the succession of notes Do - Re - Mi - Fa - Sol - La - Si - Do, in relation to the transformations that the materials present in the universe undergo, clearly shows us how these transformations proceed. Now you have to consider each musical note as a point that indicates the exact situation of any process in progress. Let us again take as an example the process of transformation which all substances present in the universe undergo. Examining all the points of the octave, that is all the notes, we will observe how the process we are considering evolves. The whole octave, that is the succession of notes Do - Re - Mi - Fa - Sol - La - Si - Do, in relation to the transformations that the materials present in the universe undergo, clearly shows us how these transformations proceed. Now you have to consider each musical note as a point that indicates the exact situation of any process in progress. Let us again take as an example the process of transformation which all substances present in the universe undergo. Examining all the points of the octave, that is all the notes, we will observe how the process we are considering evolves. it shows us clearly how these transformations proceed. Now you have to consider each musical note as a point that indicates the exact situation of any process in progress. Let us again take as an example the process of transformation which all substances present in the universe undergo. Examining all the points of the octave, that is all the notes, we will observe how the process we are considering evolves. it shows us clearly how these transformations proceed. Now you have to consider each musical note as a point that indicates the exact situation of any process in progress. Let us again take as an example the process of transformation which all substances present in the universe undergo. Examining all the points of the octave, that is all the notes, we will observe how the process we are considering evolves.

Do Re Make Me Sol You Do

1/1 - 9/8 - 5/4 - 4/3 - 3/2 - 5/3 - 18/5 - 2/1 (Reports)

1 - 1.25 - 1.25 - 1.33 - 1.5 - 1.66 - 1.75 - 2
(Frequency per second)

The first thing that immediately jumps to the eyes is that the process does not happen uniformly, it does not happen at the same speed.

between King and Do we get 9/8 divided 1/1 = 9/8 = 1,125
between Mi and Re we get 5/4 divided by 9/8 = 10/9 = 1,111
between Fa and I we obtain 4/3 divided by 5/4 = 16/15 = 1,066
between Sol and Fa we obtain 3/2 divided by 4/3 = 9/8 = 1,125
between La and Sol we get 5/3 divided by 3/2 = 10/9 = 1,111
between Si and La we get 15/8 divided by 5/3 = 9/8 = 1,125
between Do and Si we obtain 2/1 divided by 15/8 = 16/15 = 1,066

It is enough to have learned to count to ten to understand that 1,125 is greater than the number 1,111 and that the latter is greater than the number 1,066. We have found that the major slowdowns in the development of any process in any scale are placed at two precise points. The first between Mi and Fa and the second between Si and Do. As you can see for yourself, these two intervals gave the number 1,066 as a result. In fact, these two intervals correspond on the piano keyboard to the points where the black key, the so-called semitone, is missing. In these intervals the processes undergo a significant slowdown and can not continue without external help. All the other steps of the process can continue with the help of the semitones (black keys), while in the two points where the progression of the processes suffers the most noticeable slowdown (1,066) and the semitones (black keys) are missing, the process can not continue without external help, without the intervention of a lateral octave that intersecting those points helps the Mi to pass to Fa, and the Si to pass to Do. What do these slowdown points mean in processes? The formula revealed by this law shows that all the processes that occur in the universe need an external help to be able to develop completely, otherwise in the points between Mi and Fa, and between Si and Do, deviations occur in the original line, in this way the process continuously deviating, is found to proceed in the opposite direction to the initial one. In other words, a process begins with Do, continues to the King through the black semitone, from the King passes to Mi thanks to the second black semitone, but arrived at the Mi, if an external help does not intervene (the famous additional shock), then the process goes backwards until it returns to the starting Do. The process can not proceed after the Mi and therefore can not be fully achieved. If in an acoustically isolated room we make a piano according to the natural intonation and play the note Mi or the note Si, the vibrations of these notes will cease very soon compared to the others, precisely because of the principle we have just explained; therefore, the Mi will return to the Do, while the Si will come down and arrive at the Fa, it will cease to vibrate. We reiterate that all existing processes are subjected to the action of the law of the octave: from the transformation processes of all chemical substances, to the processes of transformation that the machines themselves undergo (stars, planets, plants, human beings, etc.), arising, growing, aging and eventually dying, to the processes that occur in our physical and psycho-emotional sphere, that is, the process of associations automatic thoughts and emotions, like all the metabolic processes of the body, the process of birth, progress and decline of civilizations, up to the processes of evolution or internal involution. Everything is moving, if something does not evolve, it necessarily will involute, it will be forced to degenerate. All processes, none excluded, are determined by the law of the octave. Now you can well understand that it is thanks to these breakpoints that the various processes in the universe are connected to each other. Otherwise, as shown, they could not take place. Vice versa, these same points of interruption or slowing of vibrations, if they are not filled, determine the failure of any process, as often happens in our lives, and we, instead of understanding that everything that happens is the result of these cosmic laws, we complain in vain; it is the equivalent of a man who, absurdly, not knowing the force of gravity, opening his hand and dropping an object, complained of the fall. If we now return to considering the processes of transformation that take place in the whole universe and take as an example the human being as a transforming machine of substances, we will see what follows. The materials that make up the food enter the human machine. These materials, once you enter our machine, they begin to undergo a process of evolutionary and involutive transformation; we will consider the evolutionary one, following the points Do, Re, Mi. Once they arrive at the Mi, at this point of evolution, they could not be further transformed without the help of another distinct process, that is an external octave (an extra shock), which in this case is constituted by the air we breathe.

The air entering the organism joins the Mi and helps it to continue. In this way, the transformation proceeds, Fa, Sol, La, Si. (Since this progression of notes, as you know well, or at least hopefully, implies an increase in frequency, at the same time, means that the subjects in question are becoming thinner, they are becoming less dense, therefore more alive and more intelligent). You could have noticed that this first external help happened automatically (mechanically). The entrance of the octave of the air at the point between Mi and Fa of the octave of food, happens without you doing anything, it happens automatically. Even if you are sleeping in a full-sleep bed, the air comes in and goes to fill the slow-down at that point in the process of food evolution. At the next slowdown point, however, that between Si and Do, it is necessary that the help be voluntary, that is, a conscious act on our part, otherwise the substances can not undergo further transformation into even more subtle matters, which are then the subjects that will form our second body, or astral body. This conscious act consists in being present when we receive impressions from the outside world. Impressions constitute another series of subjects (or nurturing) that enter through the sensory apparatus. The moment we look at the octave in the opposite direction, ie Do - Si - La - Sol - Fa - Mi - Re - Do, we are referring to an involutional process. Remember the example of escalators? The involutionary process represents the increase in density of the substances initially located at a high point of the scale are rendered coarser as they pass through the machines. The involutionary process is equivalent to the process of creating the universe. To get a simple idea of how creation takes place, we will take the example of a "ray" of white light that, passing through a prism, is subdivided into 7 "colored rays". The "ray" of white light will be the verb of God, the logos, its emanation, and we consider God as an astronomical body (absolute sun) around which all galaxies rotate. God emanates his creative ray, this ray is refracted and breaks up into seven colored "rays". These seven "colored rays" correspond to the 7 cosmic scales contained one inside the other like a matryoshka and made up of the absolute (Do), all the galaxies (Si), our galaxy (La), our Sun (Sol), and so on. In this case, it is good to observe another aspect of the law of sects. The law of the seven, through the principle of scale, also determines the place that occupies everything in the universe. Seven scales are thus produced one inside the other. The example of the ray of white light, which is refracted in the prism is broken down into seven colors, confirms what we said above, namely that the law of the seven is a fundamental cosmic law that dominates any process. As you can see, the visible electromagnetic spectrum is also determined by the law of sects. We have therefore seen the action of this cosmic law in the field of music, now we find it in the much higher vibrations compared to acoustic vibrations. The law of the octave is also the internal structure of everything that exists. Thus, even in this type of vibration, we find the same law that governs music. Red (Do), Orange (Re), Yellow (Mi), Green (Fa), Cyan (Sol), Blue (La), Violet (Si). The frequencies are innumerable times higher than the acoustic ones, we are in the order of Tera Hertz. The law of the seven also governs the chemical elements of the periodic table that are almost in an octave ratio, as the chemist John Newlands had guessed, but was derided by the scientific community, and the inaccuracy of atomic weights is due to an error in the modern chemistry. Another way to portray creation is the image of an inverted tree, whose roots placed at the top, represent the original source, God, the absolute. The trunk represents the cosmic fundamental octave. The branches are the secondary, tertiary octaves, the parallel octaves that are created from the fundamental octave, up to the leaves, and in the same leaves we observe the veins that are as many additional octaves. The concentric rings of the trunk, will represent various types of materials of different density that interpenetrate each other. Any gross matter is penetrated by a subtler matter, which in turn is penetrated by other even finer materials, and so on, to a certain degree. The concentric rings of the trunk will be the inner octaves. Many mistakenly associate the inner octaves with the natural harmonics, but in reality, there is a noticeable difference. Natural harmonics are multiple frequencies of a fundamental sound that propagate only in the air until the initial force that produced them is exhausted. The inner octaves, however, are vibrations that are produced in the air and at the same time also in the finest materials that penetrate the air, for this reason the Bukharian dervish Hadij-Asvatz-Truv calls it "creative vibrations", while it reserves for ordinary vibrations and to their natural harmonics the expression of "inertial vibrations". These two denominations, if you have carefully followed the speech we have previously done, already explain everything very clearly. A single note on a plane of subjects of a certain density is a whole octave on an upper plane consisting of a set of subtler materials compared to the previous plan. Another aspect of the law of the octave is that each note can represent a cosmic concentration of any kind and on any scale. For example, a sun can be represented as Do.

It is good to note now that if we consider the white ray as Do, we realize that each note contains within itself a complete octave (the 7 colored rays). At this point it is indispensable to realize that by means of the law of the seven it is possible to understand the unity of everything, unity in multiplicity.

The intervals where there are the slow-downs that require the help of another external and distinct process that when connected with the first allow its further development, are what determine the precise interdependence between each distinct thing in the universe. Through this law it is possible to understand how everything is connected with another and which place each occupies in the cosmic order. We can understand the unity of everything. This is the capital difference between objective science and current science or subjective science. Objective science has the knowledge and profound understanding of the principles that created multiplicity, and the same principles that created multiplicity allow us to understand the unity of all that exists. This chapter was an attempt to adapt to the understanding of those who approached these ideas for the first time, find it difficult to grasp the principles of this objective science. However, novice readers and those who have long ago attempted to understand these laws unsuccessfully, must understand that, although attempts can be made to simplify these laws, without much effort on their part, it will not be It is possible to penetrate the essence of these principles. The first step is to understand these laws well at a theoretical level. Then, it will be necessary to make an effort to observe their action in the outside world and, to a greater extent, in our inner world, since by being able to observe them within us, it will be easier to observe them in the external world. Finally, it is indispensable keep in mind that a person who does not know or who knows these laws has not fully understood it, can never understand the essence of any phenomenon that he observes, both in the external world and in his inner world. Such a man can only have the illusion of understanding.

Chapter 6 - Science confirms some statements by Gurdjieff

The astronomer Frederick William Herschel (1738-1822) had already affirmed at the time that the Sun is hot outside and cold inside. Herschel's observation ability is confirmed by the fact that in 1787, he discovered Titania and Oberon, two satellites of Uranus, which for the next 25 years nobody else could observe. Then, in 1789, he also discovered Mimante and Enceladus, two satellites of Saturn. Personally I have been saying for a long time that in the book "The Tales of Beelzebub to his nephew" are explained the principles of objective science that differ greatly from the ordinary conceptions of current science.

In a chapter of his work, Gurdjieff makes the following statements: "Not only does the Sun arrive neither" light ", nor" heat ", nor anything like it, but just the sun, considered" source of light and heat ", it is almost always cold and icy, like the famous bald dog of our venerable Mullah Nassr Eddin.

In reality, the surface of that "source of heat", just like the surface of all the ordinary Suns of our Great Universe, is covered with ice perhaps even more than what they cal "North Pole". [...] Although millions and millions of scientists have appeared there in every time and place, no one has ever thought that between the two cosmic phenomena called respectively "emanation" and "radiation" there is any difference. "

The Italian researcher Renzo Boscoli, more recently, has expressed similar ideas: "At the same time, while thanks to my engineer's friend my modest culture on the" official sun "was consolidating, little by little I was building in my mind a "Cold sun", revolutionary and heretical! ".

Apparently, the statements in the aforementioned work by Gurdjieff, which to some people lacking in understanding, seemed too bizarre to be taken literally and had, therefore, interpreted them imaginatively, giving them the most absurd allegorical explanations, are now confirmed by science . Here's what the scientists found. In an article published July 16, 1986 by Corriere della Sera and entitled "For the first time seen to be born a star", it read: "This object had also appeared unusual as it produced 20 times more energy than the Sun, while being incredibly cold (196 degrees below zero against 4,892 above zero of the surface of the Sun). "

Chapter 7 - True psychology and the secrets of inner practice

Everyone is able to easily verify that the constant flow of thoughts and emotions takes place automatically, in the same way that all the functions of the body are performed, from heartbeat to digestion. To a series of thoughts that revolve around a specific question, others follow completely disconnected from the previous ones. One emotion is replaced by another. Every thought and emotion constitutes a force endowed with a variable intensity. When the flow of thoughts and emotions becomes excessively unbearable, that is when the friction produced by forces at a given moment takes on a remarkable intensity, an automatic defense mechanism is activated that leads us to change external conditions. And so, we leave the house, meet a friend to talk with, we drink a few beers, someone uses drugs, we go in search of sex, or maybe we decide it's time to take a trip to visit new places and meet new people. This automatic change of external conditions, capable of modifying internal conditions, is the experimental proof that the flows of thoughts and emotions, the so-called automatic associations, are activated and modified by forces external to us and take place automatically, beyond the our will. The automatic movements of thoughts and emotions are disconnected from each other, or contradictory if of a similar nature. If disconnected, to a series of thoughts that revolved on a certain type of topic, it will follow another series that revolves around a completely different topic. If instead contradictory, a thought that affirms will oppose a thought that denies, but always within the same subject, that at that moment is the center of gravity around which the automatic associations revolve. The same dynamic will happen for the automatic flow of emotions. In addition to this, there is an interdependence between the activity of the intellect, the emotions and the body. To a given automatic flow of thoughts, the corresponding automatic flows of emotions are activated and the body takes on certain postures. When one of these flows changes, at the same time the others also change. A certain emotion corresponds to a certain posture of the body and a certain automatic flow of thoughts. In other words, they influence each other reciprocally and completely automatically. Every thought and every emotion is a force with a certain intensity, and all that we call "our actions", "our words", "our decisions", are none other than the resultant derived from the random encounter of forces endowed with different intensities, exactly as it happens in mechanics in physics. In nature, everything takes place according to causes and effects, so it is important to know how to distinguish between causes and effects, if one really wants to understand what one observes. We have clearly shown that the associative flows of thoughts and emotions are caused by forces coming from the external environment. A certain music sets in motion a certain type of automatic thoughts and emotions, the manifestations of another person, a beautiful landscape, the appearance or the atmosphere of a room, everything in us endowed with movement is moved from the outside. At this point we have already found a cause-effect relationship. The forces of the external environment cause a movement of forces within ourselves. The forces of the external environment are the cause, the movements of the forces within us are the effect. But what we consider as "our actions" are not caused by our thoughts and emotions? Without thoughts and emotions, in the ordinary state, what "action" could you ever produce? An action is a force, and like all forces it must have a cause that produced it. external environment are the cause, the movements of the forces within us are the effect. But what we consider as "our actions" are not caused by our thoughts and emotions? Without thoughts and emotions, in the ordinary state, what "action" could you ever produce? An action is a force, and like all forces it must have a cause that produced it. external environment are the cause, the movements of the forces within us are the effect. But what we consider as "our actions" are not caused by our thoughts and emotions? Without thoughts and emotions, in the ordinary state, what "action" could you ever produce? An action is a force, and like all forces it must have a cause that produced it.

Emotions and our thoughts are the indubitable motor of our "actions". Proven that the associative flow of thoughts and emotions is caused by external forces and that our "actions" are caused by our thoughts and emotions, it is easy to deduce that our actions are driven by forces from the external environment. Therefore, what we consider to be our "actions" are nothing more than automatic reactions. Man is an automaton. Everything he regards as "his thoughts", "his actions", "his emotions", are nothing but a result of the forces put into motion by the external environment. All the "actions", the thoughts, the feelings that we erroneously believe to be ours, are the equivalent of the patellar reflex produced by the percussion of the hammer below the knee. Man is not responsible for his "actions". We can not even speak of "actions" as they are real automatic reactions. Man has no will. Man can not do. Everything happens. Every force in nature always has a cause that produced it. There is no denying such a trivial principle of physics.

So, summarizing schematically:

External environment forces (CAUSA)
Associative movements of thoughts and emotions (EFFECT)

In nature every effect in turn becomes the cause of other effects, therefore, the associative movements of thoughts and emotions that are initially the effect will become the cause of our "actions". The latter is a tangible manifestation of the law of the three.

Associative movements of thoughts and emotions (CAUSA)
Our so-called "actions" (EFFECT)

It is easy to understand that our actions, by effect, will become the cause of other effects in our environment and the circle will close.
Moreover, all this talk was easy to deduce through other ways. In the universe every movement is always part of a larger movement. Every cause produces effects that in turn become causes of other effects and so on to infinity. Everything is interdependent. Everything is like a gear of a certain size that participates in the movement of the largest gears and exactly like in a clock, each gear has its own precise rhythm that is part of a larger rhythm. What we have just said is nothing but a tangible manifestation of the perpetual motion present throughout the universe. The rhythms of the body impose, at a certain time, the sensation of

hunger and push us, beyond our will, to look for food. The same happens for the sexual cycles, to which we blindly obey. A' the same thing happens on the plane of thought and emotions. Everything that happens is caused by external forces. All the instinctive automatic functions of the body, the complex automatic work that the organs of the human body perform incessantly, are nothing but a movement caused by external forces. Without these external forces, all organs would stop functioning immediately. Without external forces, the automatic flows of thoughts and emotions would stop instantly. The three external forces that produce and maintain all the movements of the body are, in order of importance: the impressions, the air we breathe and the food. Without impressions, we would die within a few seconds. Without air, we would stay alive for about 4 minutes.

Man, as we now observe him, is only a living dummy. Let's take a step back. The moment the human being comes into the world, his brains are without any registration. The same external forces that impress the recordings in its virgin ribbons of the brains, will then be the cause of the activation of that recorded material. Without these recordings, there could be no automatic association of an intellectual and emotional nature, just as no sound comes out of a virgin ribbon inserted in a cassette. In this registration process, however, an unpleasant inconvenience occurs. Through an improper education, he forms a set of records that constitute an artificial concentration and relatively separate from its totality. This concentration is erroneously called "conscious" by psychology. This fictitious conscience consists of various "I's", all fragmented that have nothing to do with each other, and each of them is activated and deactivated by external forces, when these same external forces are identical or similar in nature to those that produced it. The automatic alternation of these "I" produces corresponding automatic manifestations that have nothing conscious. in the moment when these same external forces are identical or of a similar nature to those that produced it. The automatic alternation of these "I" produces corresponding automatic manifestations that have nothing conscious. in the moment when these same external forces are identical or of a similar nature to those that produced it. The automatic alternation of these "I" produces corresponding automatic manifestations that have nothing conscious.

In this sense, the ignorance of psychology is enormous. To call conscious that which has nothing conscious is a fundamental error which affects the entire edifice of psychology. The distinction of ordinary psychology, therefore, between "conscious" and "subconscious" no longer has any real meaning. This fictitious awareness is what constitutes our personality, that is, what does not belong to us, all that has been acquired through education, culture and the environment, and which manifests itself automatically on the basis of random associations activated by forces. exterior. Where does the illusion of being conscious come from? This illusion originates from identification. By continuously identifying ourselves with the "I" which is active at that moment, we produce in ourselves the illusion that we are that particular "I" that manifests itself at a given moment. Then, the conditions change and another "I" takes the place of the previous one, and again we identify with it falling into the illusion of being ourselves that other "I" that has nothing to do with " I "previcus. You will also have a chance to observe vaguely how the tone of voice changes, your attitudes, from when you are at work to when you are at home. All these different personalities have nothing in common with each other, they are activated automatically beyond your will, and their interests and desires differ greatly. This fictitious conscience, which originated from an incorrect education and formed by a myriad of " I "fragmented" who do not communicate with each other, who do not know each other thanks to the formation of the "repugnants", prevents our true "I" who lives in what is called "subconscious" to participate in activities of the entire psycho-emotional sphere. The real evolution corresponds to a growth of the essence. The essence is what we really are, what belongs to us. On the other hand, personality is useful only in life in society. Just as every thought and emotion constitutes a force, so each of these "I" is a force, and since they are different from each other, they are contradictory, the possible contact between these opposing forces, would create an unbearable inner friction, therefore, for this reason they are formed " it teaches that any phenomenon can occur only when three forces come into play. The law of the three and the natural constitution of man, which is made up of three brains, make us understand that man can be the creator of his actions, man can really do, he can move the cause from the outside to the inside of himself, only when all three of his brains participate simultaneously in the overall activity. The simultaneous action of his three brains, according to the law of the three, can produce the phenomena we call "will", "conscience", "inner unity". To animals, by constitution, being unicerebral or bicerebral, this possibility is denied. A Man, in the true sense of the word, therefore, is a being in which his three brains work simultaneously, a being with all three cute brains. Until this happens, until man is in a given intellectual instant, in another emotional moment, man remains a cow, a worm, a giraffe, or a simple animal with one or two brains, which he eats, it reproduces and sleeps. Therefore, the one who is preparing himself for a real and correct inner practice must immediately understand that the first step consists in starting from what is within his reach. All the discussions that concern spiritual conditions that are inaccessible and extremely far from what constitutes their current being, must be abolished in the most categorical way. Speaking of conscience, awareness and enlightenment is an absolutely useless and counterproductive activity in view of a real inner practice. Real practice will consist in knowing oneself. If a man does not know himself, no other thing is possible. Self-observation is necessary to know oneself. One who will try to observe himself will realize that he is not capable of attention.

His attention is continually drawn to external forces acting as real magnetic forces. The man who has no attention can not observe himself, and if he can not observe himself, he will never know himself. This initial practice, if conducted correctly, will produce three results. The first result will be the experimental test that is a slave to external influences and can not even control one's attention. He will have the experimental proof that his conviction of being the architect of his actions is only an illusion, that he is not able to love, or to do anything, in him something loves, another hates, and everything happens automatically. It is fundamental for man to experience his mechanicalness, he must absolutely not believe it, he must prove it, for it is precisely in this personal verification that the practice has its real beginning. The second result will create in him the conditions for realizing his own nothingness.

A man who experiences not being the creator of his actions, his thoughts, his emotions, realizes that he is a nothingness. A man who realizes that he has no inner power, even if he is the president of the United States, realizes that he does not exist at all. The realization of one's own nullity is indispensable to make all those "I" who constitute the fictitious conscious die, so that the true "I" can be born. The man who realizes his own nothingness wakes up. The third result will consist in increasing and strengthening the attention itself through continuous and incessant attempts to obtain it. Through this practice, you will understand that already self-observation is not a simple thing, it is a distant destination. Observation of oneself and self-remembering are distant destinations, not as accessible as generally believed. Many believe they can remember themselves in some moments, while it is only a part that observes another for a few moments. True self-remembering is possible only when all three brains are awake. Those who have the illusion of being already at a good level, will have to verify with sincerity and eventually start all over again. On the other hand you will finally understand that those who believe they can know each other better by studying modern psychology are like donkeys listening to the brains of other donkeys, they delude that they have heard the gentle song of the bird of paradise. This also applies to all those who are deluding themselves that they can achieve something real through a mantra or something else, usually always cheap. There is nothing of this. Man is immersed in a hypnotic sleep, and this happens when the connections between his brains are interrupted. The real inner work produces much suffering that we have to assume and accept voluntarily, all the other practices that promise an inner evolution without "sacrifices", are charlatanas that fall in the field of suggestion and reciprocal hypnosis, precisely the opposite of the real awakening .

Chapter 8 - Mesmer, animal magnetism and scientific evidence

Two hundred years have passed since the death of Dr. Franz Anton Mesmer, however, his hopes moved by the highest and noblest sentiments have not been realized and, considering the current state of the scientific world, will hardly be seen in the future. Mesmer, among the many merits, has that of having tried to bring this knowledge, from the field of superstition in which it had been lying for centuries, to the world of science. In fact, the understanding of animal magnetism is fundamental to illuminate different fields of human knowledge in a new light, some still in the darkness of irrational superstition, while others are already part of the world of science, although very superficially understood. Astrology, demonic possessions, medicine, thaumaturgy, hypnotism, alchemy, psychology, etc., they are understood in their true essence with the help of "mesmeric science". The German physician Christoph Wilhelm Hufeland was aware of this when he declared: "On the field of vital magnetism there is a novel dawn for the. sciences and life, a discovery that surpasses what was discovered so far, which gives us the key to the deepest mysteries of nature, and opens us a whole new world. "It is good to remember that animal magnetism is an old knowledge. Through the chronicles of some historians of the past we learn of the presence of these phenomena already in different ancient civilizations and cultures. Their knowledge differed only in the method used to provoke these particular states and in the understanding they had of them. That of Mesmer, therefore, is essentially a rediscovery. On the day of today, science believes that the question of animal magnetism was already resolved in 1784, when the King of France appointed a scientific commission to study the phenomenon. The result of this verification was published in a report which, discrediting the animal magnetism, declared the non-existence of the magnetic fluid and attributed the cause of all the phenomena to the imagination and to the suggestion. In reality, the exams of this much-vaunted commission were conducted awkwardly. The examiners, already imbued with prejudice, had from the beginning decided for a negative verdict. It is not by chance that one of the members of the commission, the botanist AL de Jussieu, refused to sign the report and published another independent, illustrating the facts omitted and those that, in his opinion, had been misunderstood. But that is not all. In 1825, another scientific commission was commissioned to re-examine the phenomenon. This time the investigations were conducted with extreme seriousness and for five long years. The final report, needless to say, was positive. The verdict of the previous commission, which ascribed to the imagination and the suggestion the cause of the magnetic phenomena, was completely refuted through various experiments that demonstrated the manifestation of the "magnetic effects" on the nervous system of subjects totally ignorant of being magnetized, therefore absolutely out of any possible contact that could induce suggestion. It is necessary to understand that the discovery of animal magnetism disturbed, not a little, first of all the doctors of the time and secondly, the church and the holders of political power. Some doctors openly affirmed their fear of seeing Mesmer's method recognized, as it undermined the very foundations of all established conceptions of medicine. One of these doctors wondered if they should eventually burn all the books that had formed the foundation of medical science. Secondly, there was the church that had always exploited and marched triumphantly over the ignorance and superstitions of the people and in seeing themselves illuminate all the dark phenomena, from demonic possession to ecstatic visions to so-called miracles, from the light of this new science , he became alarmed and through various publications, he threw the anathema against the magnetizers. Some doctors openly affirmed their fear of seeing Mesmer's method recognized, as it undermined the very foundations of all established conceptions of medicine. One of these doctors wondered if they should eventually burn all the books that had formed the foundation of medical science. Secondly, there was the church that had always exploited and marched triumphantly over the ignorance and superstitions of the people and in seeing themselves illuminate all the dark phenomena, from demonic possession to ecstatic visions to so-called miracles, from the light of this new science , he became alarmed and through various publications, he threw the anathema against the magnetizers. Some doctors openly affirmed their fear of seeing Mesmer's method recognized, as it undermined the very foundations of all established conceptions of medicine. One of these doctors wondered if they should eventually burn all the books that had formed the foundation of medical science. Secondly, there was the church that had always exploited and marched triumphantly over the ignorance and superstitions of the people and in seeing themselves illuminate all the dark phenomena, from demonic possession to ecstatic visions to so-called miracles, from the light of this new science , he became alarmed and through various publications, he threw the anathema against the magnetizers. One of these doctors wondered if they should eventually burn all the books that had formed the foundation of medical science. Secondly, there was the church that had always exploited and marched triumphantly over the ignorance and superstitions of the people and in seeing themselves illuminate all the dark phenomena, from demonic possession to ecstatic visions to so-called miracles, from the light of this new science , he became alarmed and through various publications, he threw the anathema against the magnetizers. One of these doctors wondered if they should eventually burn all the books that had formed the foundation of medical science. Secondly, there was the church that had always exploited and marched triumphantly over the ignorance and superstitions of the people and in seeing themselves illuminate all the dark phenomena, from demonic possession to ecstatic visions to so-called miracles, from the light of this new science , he became alarmed and through various publications, he threw the anathema against the magnetizers.

The Flemish chemist, physiologist and physician Jean Baptiste van Helmont, about 150 years before Mesmer, already declared: "Magnetism acts everywhere and has nothing else but the name; it is not a paradox if not for those who laugh at everything, and who attribute to the power of Satanasso what they can not explain ". Finally, even the holders of political power were alarmed, as is evident from the statements made by the French prince, bishop and politician Charles Maurice de Talleyrand-Périgord: "Mesmer was, when I met him at Voltaire, a German doctor. It was said that he had found the existence of magnetic fluid, property of the body, a phenomenon still almost unknown, but whose strength of truth obliges me to recognize its existence. This fluid, one of whose faculties is to determine artificial somnambulism much more tenacious than the real, produces, in the opinion of Mesmer and its members, such extraordinary effects as to confuse reason. Instead of trying to lighten up this curious and important fact, he cried out, as usual, against charlatanism; but as for me I will say frankly that I have seen such miracles operated by magretism, that my intellect is frightened by the corsequences which it would be necessary to deduce from it. I would like science, laying down the contempt with which it accepted the circulation of blood, the transfusion of metals, the antimony, the electricity, the inoculation of the vaccine, and recently the steam, gave spirit to clear the question and to observe it with solemn experiences and all of good faith. I made a proposal to Napoleon about this: he listened to me carefully, thought for a long time, then said to me: "No, we do not make somnambulism a legal thing, consider what would become the politics of toilets! quiet of the public, for the secret of families this science remains vague, contrasted, even ridiculous: each one will earn you what they would all lose to you ". As a consequence of all this, we note that the rejection by the scientific community has allowed this important discovery to end up in the hands of general ignorance, favoring its use and abuse. The result is extremely evident when we see the acrobats appearing ridiculous antics in which pots and lids are glued on the body, claiming to possess a "magnetic power" that allows him to perform such prodigies. Then, books are published that announce the revelation of the secrets of this art, and perhaps with the help of courses and lectures, the authors of these absurdities, they earn the bread by exploiting the ingenuity of others. The authors of these books, in fact, treat the subject without any baggage of serious knowledge, with an impressive superficiality and in their imaginative and imaginative ruminations often confuse animal magnetism with the magnetic fields of physics. In this regard, the words of Mesmer come back to mind: "Animal magnetism is absolutely not what doctors mean when they think of a secret medicine. It is a science that has its causes, its effects, its laws. Protected by my honesty, I will gather around me a small part of that humanity to which I had wished to benefit, and at that point the hour will come when I will not ask for advice on what to do except to myself. If I did otherwise, animal magnetism could turn into a fashion. Everyone would try to be nice with it and to find, at their own convenience, more or less what is really there. This would result in an abuse and its actual usefulness could degenerate into a problem whose solution would perhaps be impossible only after centuries. "The current tremendous confusion between animal magnetism and magnetism already known to physics is sufficient proof of incompetence. Mesmer, in his time, complained of those who confounded animal magnetism with mineral magnetism, spread the error that complicated even more the whole question. In fact, numerous experiments proved to be a completely new agent that did not interfere with magnetism of the magnet or compass needle, as it was sensed by the nervous system of the subjects and produced evident effects of various types. The decision to call it "animal magnetism" is due to the fact that similarities were presented with mineral magnetism, such as two distinct polarities, etc. After all, if it were the magnetic fields known to physics, there would be no difficulty in identifying them through adequate equipment and tools. Instead, it is precisely in this sense that difficulties arise, since this "magnetic fluid" is an unknown matter and of such a density, that it can not be detected by any instrument hitherto built by man. Only the sensitivity of the human nervcus system is able to receive it adequately and reacting accordingly, manifests the tangible effects to the scientist who deviates from prejudices can prepare to study it. So, it is legitimate to ask: is not the nervous system itself a more than valid detection tool?

The answer is affirmative, however, prejudices combined with fear and ignorance, condemned Mesmer to interminable slander and finally to oblivion. I confess that it makes a certain impression to observe that the well-known arms manufacturer Alfred Bernhard Nobel is called a philanthropist, while to Dr. Mesmer, who has dedicated his whole life to the good of humanity, is reserved the undeserved and totally unjustified reputation of charlatan and, at best, that of a visionary. In reference to all this, Gurdjieff's comment is lapidary: "The more wise men of that original planet are idiots squared, more critical of Mesmer telling and writing about him absurdities of any kind intended to denigrate.

In 1825, a scientific study demonstrated the existence of animal magnetism. This enlightening scientific report, published in 1833 by MP Foissac, is still publicly available thanks to the precious work of the American Society of Anesthesiologists who, through the Wood Library-Museum of Anesthesiology, a precious online library, aims to collect, preserve and make accessible to anyone, the scientific works related to anesthesiology, even the most unobtainable and rare. Current science, as we mentioned in the introduction, believes that the question of animal magnetism is closed, and to close it was a commission of scientists in 1784. History shows us that when a theory has been refuted in a definitive way, not more experimentations are undertaken to verify it. No one would dream today to conduct experiments to demonstrate a theory that states that the Sun revolves around the Earth. It's a closed affair. We all know that the Copernican theory has been verified, and it would be absurd to conduct experiments in this sense. The very existence of a new commission in 1825, after forty-one years, able to verify again the theory of animal magnetism, shows that the question had not been satisfactorily resolved by the commission of 1784. There was even one of the members of this commission , the botanist AL de Jussieu, who categorically refused to sign the final report, and in the same year published a separate report where he talked about some facts that were deliberately not included in the report. This shows that there was already a background prejudice in the study committee scientists. This verification, in effect, was conducted absently and resolved in a very short time, as if to immediately liquidate the matter. This scientific disaster was published in 1784 and titled: Rapport des Commissaires de la Société Royale de Médecine, Nommés par le roi pour faire the Examen du Magnétisme

Animal. The botanist AL de Jussieu, not sharing this relationship, published the same year his separate report: Rapport de l'un des Commissaires Chargés par le Roi de l'Examen du Magnétisme Animal - AL de Jussieu (1784). We are in 1825, when Dr. Foissac asked the Paris Academy of Medicine to attend some experiments aimed at producing some phenomena by means of animal magnetism. The Academy, in the uncertainty of accepting the invitation or not, assigned the task of evaluating this request to an appropriate commission. The Commission composed of Adelon, Pariset, Marc, Burdin and Husson, he decided affirmatively. The Academy therefore constituted another commission, entrusting it with the study of animal magnetism. This commission was composed of: Bourdois de la Motte, Fouquier, Gueneau de Mussy, Guersant, Hard, Leroux, Marc, Thillaye, Husson. Five long years of investigations, studies and experiments finally demonstrated the reality of animal magnetism and the effects produced by it. The enormous final report of 561 pages, the result of five long years of testing and experimentation, was published in 1833 by MP Foissac. This document called "Rapports et discussions de l'Académie Royale de Médecine sur le Magnetisme Animal", needless to underline, was positively pronounced. entrusting it with the study of animal magnetism. This commission was composed of: Bourdois de la Motte, Fouquier, Gueneau de Mussy, Guersant, Hard, Leroux, Marc, Thillaye, Husson. Five long years of investigations, studies and experiments finally demonstrated the reality of animal magnetism and the effects produced by it. The enormous final report of 561 pages, the result of five long years of testing and experimentation, was published in 1833 by MP Foissac. This document called "Rapports et discussions de l'Académie Royale de Médecine sur le Magnetisme Animal", needless to underline, was positively pronounced. entrusting it with the study of animal magnetism. This commission was composed of: Bourdois de la Motte, Fouquier, Gueneau de Mussy, Guersant, Hard, Leroux, Marc, Thillaye, Husson. Five long years of investigations, studies and experiments finally demonstrated the reality of animal magnetism and the effects produced by it. The enormous final report of 561 pages, the result of five long years of testing and experimentation, was published in 1833 by MP Foissac. This document called "Rapports et discussions de l'Académie Royale de Médecine sur le Magnetisme Animal", needless to underline, was positively pronounced. they finally demonstrated the reality of animal magnetism and the effects produced by it. The enormous final report of 561 pages, the result of five long years of testing and experimentation, was published in 1833 by MP Foissac. This document called "Rapports et discussions de l'Académie Royale de Médecine sur le Magnetisme Animal", needless to underline, was positively pronounced. they finally demonstrated the reality of animal magnetism and the effects produced by it. The enormous final report of 561 pages, the result of five long years of testing and experimentation, was published in 1833 by MP Foissac. This document called "Rapports et discussions de l'Académie Royale de Médecine sur le Magnetisme Animal", needless to underline, was positively pronounced. The conclusions of this long and accurate study are presented in the Husson report that we present below.

Conclusions of the Husson report

1. The contact of the thumbs or hands, the frictions or certain gestures that are made at a short distance from the body, and which are called past (passes), are the means used to put in relation, or in other words to transmit the action magnetized magnetizer.

2. The external and visible means are not always necessary, since, on many occasions, the will, the gaze fixed enough to produce the magnetic phenomena, even without the knowledge of the

magnetized. (This second conclusion is very important to demonstrate the incompetence of the first commission when it stated that it was all a matter of imagination and suggestion.The magnetic phenomena also occurred through procedures carried out without the knowledge of the subjects.)

3. Magnetism acted on people of different ages and ages.

4. The time required to transmit and let the magnetic action prove varied from one hour to one minute.

5. Magnetism does not generally act on people who enjoy healthy health. (This fifth point confirms what Mesmer and his pupils had long ago established: In the work "Théorie du Monde and des étres organisés suivant les princes de Mesmer", published in 1784, we read: "A body being in harmony is insensitive to the effect of animal magnetism, since the application of a uniform and general action can not change anything of the exact and already conforming

proportions of this same harmony, if on the contrary a body is no longer in harmony, that is to say if the proportions in the what must be done in him the progression of life is disturbed, it becomes sensitive to the application of animal magnetism, since this application increases in him the dissonance that he experienced before.)

6. It acts even above all the sick.

7. Sometimes, while one magnetizes, some insignificant and fleeting effects that we do not attribute to magnetism alone, like a bit of oppression, of heat or cold, or some other nervous phenomena, which can be realized without resort to the intervention of a particular agent; that is, for the hope or the fear, the prevention and the expectation of something new and unknown, the boredom resulting from the monotony of gestures, the silence and the rest maintained during the experience, and finally the imagination which exercises a so much power over certain minds and certain organizations.

8. A number of the observed effects seemed to depend on magnetism alone, and did not reproduce without it. They are well established physiological and therapeutic phenomena.

9. The real effects produced by magnetism are very different! It agitates some, calms others, often causes a momentary acceleration of breathing and circulation, of convulsive passenger movements, resembling electric shocks, a more or less deep numbness, drowsiness, drowsiness, and in a small number of cases , what magnetizers name sleepwalking.

10. The existence of a single character, precisely to make recognizing, in all cases, the reality of a state of somnambulism, was not established.

11. Nevertheless it can be concluded with certainty that such a state exists, when it gives rise to the unfolding of new faculties that were designated under the names of clairvoyance, intuition, internal prediction, and that it produces great changes in the physiological state. , like insensitivity, a sudden and considerable increase

in strength, and this effect can not be referred to another cause.

12. As among the effects attributed to somnambulism, there are some that can be simulated, sleepwalking can also sometimes be simulated, and to provide the charlatans with the means of deception. Therefore, in the observation of these phenomena, which do not yet appear as isolated facts, which can not be approximated to any theory, it is only with the most careful examination, the most severe precautions, and by means of numerous and varied tests. that you can escape the illusion.

13. Sleep caused with greater or less readiness, and established in a more or less profound degree, is a real, but not constant, effect of magnetism.

14. It has been shown to us that it was provoked also in circumstances in which the magnetized ones could not see the means employed to produce it, and ignored them. (And this reconfirms what has been said before, or that the

cause of the phenomena produced can not be attributed to imagination and suggestion)

15. When someone once let a person in magnetic sleep enter, he does not always need to resort to contact and the past to magnetize him again. The magnetist's gaze, his sole will have the same influence on that person. In this case it can not only act on the magnetized, but also put it completely in sleepwalking, Sorting and do it without his knowledge, out of his view, at a certain distance, and through closed doors. (Once the magnetic contact is established, the subject is literally under the power of the magnetizer even if he acts at a distance and through the walls.Please the reader to meditate deeply on the implications of the phenomena observed by these scientists)

16. Ordinarily there are more or less noticeable changes in the perceptions and faculties of individuals who enter sleepwalking as a result of magnetism.

a) Some amid the noise of confused conversations, they do not mean the voice of their magnetizer; many answer in a precise way to the questions that this, or the people with whom they were put in relation, they direct; others converse with all the people around them, but it is rare that they understand what is going on around them. Generally they are by no means inaccessible to the external and unexpected noise that is made to their ear, such as the din of strongly beaten copper vessels, the fall of a piece of furniture, etc.

b) The eyes are closed, the eyelids hardly yield to the efforts made by hands to open them. This operation, which is not without pain, allows the eye of the convulsive eye to be seen and generally aimed at the top, sometimes at the bottom of the orbit.

c) Sometimes the smell is like annihilated. You can make them inhale muriatic acid or ammonia without them being disturbed, without them having the slightest hint. In some cases the opposite occurs, and is sensitive to odors.

d) Most of the sleepwalkers we saw were completely unresponsive. They were able to tickle their feet, nostrils, and the angle of the eyes with the feather of a pen, to pinch the skin in an echimosarla, to sting under the nail with pins stuck suddenly to a considerable depth, without having given any sign of pain, without having noticed it. Finally there was one that remained insensitive to a surgical operation of the most painful, while neither the face, the pulse nor the breathing gave a sign of the slightest emotion.

17. Magnetism has the same intensity, it is so promptly affected by the distance of six feet, as of six inches, and the phenomena to which it gives rise are the same in both cases. (A real influence at a distance.) Now try to think how many unconscious influences occur among people by means of this subtle magnetic fluid and in ignorance they call these phenomena with

meaningless names, namely: empathy, antipathy, attraction, repulsion, love, hate, etc. Imagine that leaps from giants would make psychology if its study were founded on these principles.We would certainly have a totally different psychology, instead of the classic ruminations.)

18. Action at a distance does not seem to be able to successfully exercise that above individuals have already been subjected to magnetization at other times.

19. We have never seen that a magnetized person for the first time fell into sleepwalking; it was not until the eighth, the tenth session that somnambulism appeared.

20. We constantly saw the ordinary sleep, which is the rest of the sense organs, of the intellectual faculties and of the voluntary motions, to precede and end the state of sleepwalking.

21. During sleepwalking, the magnetized we have observed preserve the exercise of the faculties that they possess in the wake. Their memory seems even more faithful and more extensive,

since they are overwhelmed by what happened in all the time and in all the times they were in sleepwalking.

22. Upon their awakening they say they have completely obliterated all circumstances of the sleepwalking state, and never give it up. We can not have other guarantees in this regard than their declaration.

23. The muscular forces of the sleepwalkers are sometimes numb and paralyzed; other times the movements are not impeded, and the sleepwalkers walk or waver in the manner of drunken men, and without avoiding, sometimes even avoiding, the obstacles they encounter in their passage. There are somnambulists who keep the exercise of their movements intact, they are also seen of those who are stronger and more agile than in the waking state.

24. We have seen sleepwalkers distinguish with their eyes closed the objects that were placed before them; they designated, without touching them, the color and value of the cards, read of

the words written by hand, or some lines of books that they were presented open to gambling. This phenomenon also took place when the opening of the eyelids was kept closed with the fingers. (point 24 suggests the existence of a sensory apparatus more sensitive than that of the physical body, and perhaps belonging to the astral body)

25. In two sleepwalkers we found the ability to foresee acts of the organism, more or less distant, more or less complicated. One of them announced many days, many months before, the day, hour and minute of the invasion and the return of epileptic accesses; the other indicated the exact period of his recovery. Their predictions were realized with remarkable accuracy. These seemed to us to be able to refer only to acts or injuries of their organism.

26. We found only one sleepwalker who indicated the symptoms of the three-person illness with whom she had been interconnected. Although we have investigated a large enough number.

27. In order to establish the relationship of magnetism with the therapeutic rightly, one should have observed its effects on a great number of individuals, and have had long and daily experiences of the same sick. This having not taken place, the Commission had to limit itself to saying what it saw in too few cases, without daring to decide.

28. Some of the magnetized patients were not affected by it; others experienced a more or less marked improvement, that is: someone's suppression of habitual pains, the other the restoration of strength, a third the delay of many months in the appearance of epileptic fits, and a fourth complete recovery from a paralysis serious and inveterate.

29. Considered as an agent of physiological phenomena or as a therapeutic means, magnetism should find its place within the framework of medical knowledge; and consequently physicians alone should make or

monitor their use, as practiced in the countries of the North.

30. The Commission could not verify, because it had no opportunity, other faculties which the magnetizers had announced existed in the sleepwalkers; but it gathered and communicated facts that were important enough to think that the Academy should encourage investigations into magnetism as a very unique branch of psychology and natural history.

In 1815, the emperor of Russia also appointed a commission to study the phenomena produced by animal magnetism.

The commission concluded that it was a very important agent and it was essential that it be used only by experienced doctors. Some of the phenomena and faculties that were manifested in cases of somnambulism caused by animal magnetism, observed and documented by numerous doctors.

1) Physical Insensitivity: not only to the skin, but also in the subcutaneous tissues, in the muscles and even in the nervous ramifications.

2) Vision without the aid of the eyes: the vision through the closed eyelids, through the opaque bodies, in the most complete darkness without the intervention of light and even at enormous distances is not only a real fact, but a very frequent phenomenon.

3) Intuition to the Maximum Degree of Perfection: time, space, forces of all kinds, resistance and gravity of objects are measured, calculated, evaluated at a single stroke.

4) Internal Forecast: the lucid somnambulists have not only the awareness of their current physiological or pathological state, but also announce with a kind of prescience all the modifications that will have to take place in their organism.

5) External Forecast: some individuals have the faculty to predict in their sleepwalking events that will affect their existence.

6) Penetration of Thought: the ability of some sleepwalkers to penetrate the thoughts of the people around them. The communication of thought from the magnetizer to the magnetized.

7) Transposition of the Senses: some saw, felt, tasted and heard through the stomach, at the ends of the fingers or with the feet.

Many experiments clearly demonstrate the existence of an unknown subtle matter. The seven listed phenomena would easily be explained by introducing the existence of a subtle body provided with a sensory apparatus that is considerably more sensitive than that of the physical body, or considering the so-called higher centers mentioned by Gurdjieff. Animal magnetism opens the door to a much deeper knowledge of the human being.

This knowledge would also extend to the universe, and we would understand how absurd a conception is that admits the existence of emptiness that makes impossible, except through imaginary theories, the explanation, for example, of phenomena such as gravity. Recognizing what the experiments have shown, that is, the existence of a series of unknown and much more subtle subjects than those hitherto known, would allow us to acquire a greater understanding of man and the universe. The following is a translation from French of a chapter on gravity and taken from the work published in 1784, "Théorie du monde et des êtres organisés suivant les principes de Mesmer", which demonstrates how the knowledge of animal magnetism is able to provide a

Of Gravity

Everything is done by transmission in Nature. The attractions or impulses and repulsions that are observed are not that apparent. The cause of the apparent attraction, or of impulse and repulsion, is between the incoming and outgoing currents of the universal fluid. An incoming current can not exist without an outgoing current, since everything is full in the universe. It has been said that there is a mutual tendency among all the coexisting bodies in space, this tendency is called gravity. Therefore all bodies gravitate towards each other. It has been said that the tendency of bodies is because of their masses and their distances. Therefore all bodies gravitate towards each other because of their masses and their distances. It has been said that the cause of the tendency of bodies is in the currents in which they are immersed. Therefore the currents in which the bodies are immersed are the cause of gravity. Attraction does not exist in nature, it is only apparent. A general current of the elementary subtle matter or of the universal fluid directs itself towards the center of any globe, dragging in its direction all the combined matter it encounters and which is why it is combined, and opposes a resistance. The more the resistance of the combined material opposes the current is considerable and the greater the speed with which this matter is drawn in the direction of the current. The precipitation of the combined material has therefore been made due to the resistance of each of its particles. The grossest of these particles therefore precipitated first. Thus all the layers of matter were formed, that make up our globe. Thus all the layers of matter that make up the different globes have been formed. The amount of the effect of gravity is called heaviness. The driving force of a current is applied to each of the dragging molecules, the amount of the effect of gravity or the heaviness is due to the velocity of the current and the resistance of the particles, ie the more the particles are coarse and the rapid current is the more the particles are heavy. The velocity of the currents grows to the extent of approaching the Earth, as they become more convergent, gravity increases in the same proportion. In the same way that all heavy bodies gravitate towards the Earth, the Earth gravitates towards heavy bodies and towards all its constituent parts. The cause of the gravity of the Earth to the heavy bodies and to all its constituent parts is in the currents that come out of its interstices or outgoing currents, as the cause of the gravity of heavy bodies towards the center is in the currents entering its interstices or in the re-entrant currents. The gravity of the Earth towards the heavy bodies and towards all its constituent parts is less considerable than the gravity of the heavy bodies towards the Earth because the currents that come out of the Earth are divergent and those that enter are convergent, and the outgoing currents still conserve the sinuosity that they had acquired in the interstices of the Earth while the incoming currents rush towards the Earth with greater direction. At the points where the incoming and outgoing currents are in equilibrium, gravity ceases. therefore, between the Moon and Earth, at a certain distance between these two stars, gravity ends. The currents that go from the Earth to the Moon are initially very weak and divergent, insensibly they become convergent and their rapidity increases, in the same way the currents that go from the Moon to the Earth are, at first, just as very weak and divergent, insensibly they become convergent and their speed increases. Now there must be points where the speed of some is equal to the speed of the others and in these points gravity must cease. It is for this reason that a body that will be in this place will no longer be determined to go to the Earth or to the Moon. So, even at a certain depth of the Earth's mass, gravity ends, because at a certain depth of the Earth's mass, as between the Earth and the Moon, there must also be points where the incoming currents do not predominate over the outgoing currents and where the rapidity of the ones is equal to that of the others, and at these points we can see that gravity is absent. At the center of the Earth everything must be in dissolution, because what makes one movement, the other destroys it, since the incoming and source currents are extremely joined together; therefore, due to the effect of the currents that go towards the Earth, the solidity of the Earth increases, until to a certain degree and beyond this, the fluidity must begin. and at these points we can see that gravity is absent. At the center of the Earth everything must be in dissolution, because what makes one movement, the other destroys it, since the incoming and source currents are extremely joined together; therefore, due to the effect of the currents that go towards the Earth, the solidity of the Earth increases, until to a certain degree and beyond this, the fluidity must begin. and at these points we can see that gravity is absent. At the center of the Earth everything must be in dissolution, because what makes one movement, the other destroys it, since the incoming and source currents are extremely joined together; therefore, due to the effect of the currents that go towards the Earth, the solidity of the Earth increases, until to a certain degree and beyond this, the fluidity must begin.

[...] Man is therefore subjected to all the impressions of the celestial bodies, of the earth and of particular bodies more or less like the arm of a river obeying all the impressions, to all the movements of the river to which it belongs. The faculty which in man makes it susceptible to receive impressions of the influence of the heavenly bodies, of the earth and of particular bodies is what we call Animal Magnetism. Man has penetrated from all sides by various universal currents to which he obeys. The universal and particular currents change differently in man according to the interstices they cross; that is, they acquire different tones of movement following the different organizations of the constituent parts in which they are enclosed. The fluid that constitutes the currents follows the continuity of the bodies of the man up to the most eminent parts or its extremities. In these extremities the currents come out and fall back. In these extremities the currents acquire a great velocity because they are, so to speak, restricted in a point and it is known that the more a current is restricted and the faster it becomes. All the bodies whose shape ends at the tip or at an angle are proper to receive the tonic currents and become conductors.

Chapter 9 - A woman healed by means of sleep with light vision

What follows is one of the many cases reported in the medical-scientific report published in 1842 that documents the healings obtained through unusual means by Dr. Angelo Cogevina, a surgeon and director in the Civilian Hospital of Corfu.

Adriana Zerboni, aged 28, was often hysterical assaulted convulsions. - Visit it one day (July 19, 1840 at half past eight in the morning), while he was in current convulsive access, Dr. Angelo Cogevina, wanted to try the effectiveness of Animal Magnetism, being present the Lords Deumetrio Seremeti, Demetrio Mustoxidi, and many females.

The magnetization was with our usual method of small-distance manipulations constituting the so-called high-current treatment, with a longer dwelling on the head, and on the stomach.

After 12 minutes of mesmerizing especially on the epigastrium, the magnetic sleep, and the somniloquy were manifested with great wonder of the bystanders, who in a sick glue, ignored what was done, looked at those gestures with amazement, and did not know what he wanted artifact. View the sick with the extrinsic characters of sleep, and question her if she slept - She answered immediately, - How much she wanted to sleep. - He answered an hour. Immediately afterwards, questioned several times, or by one or the other bystanders, he did not answer. "He then directed questions from the magnetizer to the subject of the evil he suffered," he said. "The seat of this being between the heart and the lung, but on that day. not being able to say more, not having the mind quite lucid. - The day after the clarity was to become greater - you had to leave it for now at rest, since sleep was good for you - so in fact it was done. Only in time she wondered if it was time to wake her up, and she always answered no, until she saw the last minute, after which she said she wanted to be woken up, so it was done.

July 20th 7 am

Magnetic sleep in one minute was produced with only the count of fingers against fingers. Then questioned his own evil - He answered. That between the heart and the lung there was a thread like a hair that adhered these two organs - That Animal Magnetism would soon have broken this thread, and then the healing would be complete, nor would the Mesmeric operations have had on her the smallest action. To other subsequent questions, although his eyes were closed, he recognized most of the bystanders by calling them in his name, and Mr. D. Spiridionie Lessi who had arrived at that moment - He said he would be able to fall asleep also magnetizing her from the next room, and that he wanted to sleep only 20 minutes. It was well isolated, and only responded to the magnetizer alone.

Day itself - 3 pm

The magnetizer sneaked into a room close to where the Zerboni was. It was in the company of Mr. Alessandro Cambissa, Mr. Mustoxidi and many women. Unbeknownst to all, he stared from the room where the place corresponding to the patient's position was in the other chamber, and directed the sonic manipulations for about five minutes on the dividing wall, after which time, to the utmost surprise of the bystanders, it fell asleep in his bed, while there he was confabulating with those present. Some of them supposed at first that a swoon had come to her. The magnetizer came in, and took everyone out of deception. He then passed to the appropriate questions, and she answered - That sleep had been caused by the velvet she wielded in the other room (so she translated the impression of the magnetic aura she resented) - Which was better. Who knew very well all the bystanders, who pointed out from hand to hand calling them in their name, though their eyes were still closed in them-that the Seremeti was about to arrive, as happened, although she could not know it by sight, nor by hearing. - Established the communication between the patient and Maria B. and questioned her patient about the health of the latter. - Answered - There is a vein that continually flows towards its wound, and that prevents healing - Asked if the remedies he used against the wound that he really had could heal it - He answered with them will never be healed - Request if they knew others more appropriate. - He replied that it was worth a much simpler cure, with which within two months he would recover if he were to be disturbed. - Asked what this cure should be. - He replied after much thought - A very simple remedy - Nothing but waxed ointment. (In fact, treated Maria B. in this way, after two months she was not healed, but she had improved her condition much more than in a whole year of other care, but some disorder made her stay in the hospice until the first July: the time has come to wake her up, very easily with a few counter-manipulations, the awakening is excellent.

Same day.

He did not recover afterwards, talking with his companions, and not being able to notice, the magnetizer entered the contiguous chamber again, as above, and reiterating the magnetic operation on the wall, in two minutes he obtained the renewal of sleep in the presence of the Doctor. I read. He was questioned immediately afterwards because he had fallen asleep. - He replied that this was due to what the Doctor had done to her in the next room. Communicating with SB and asking her what harm he had - He replied. This young man must have taken venereal diseases (so it is pertinently denied). Angered by this denial she adds - It is not possible that she has been deceived, since she sees the venereal disease running through the patient's bones, and ends with saying - Do not you see how it is fixed here? Pointing at the knee - Does not it presently present pains in the bones? - (In fact, the sick man was suffering from a genartrocace and a pain in the left coxo-femoral articulation that extended all along the sciatic nerve.) Then questioned what power to be the most appropriate means to heal it - He answered. three days of baths, and continue the decoction that takes (which was wooden guajaco) and give it every morning for five of three grains of calomelano and, after the three baths begin the friction with the belladonna in the parts where there is pain giving principle from his arms, then coming to his chest, and continuing to the other sore parts, questioned. "If he would heal perfectly with this method," he replied, "Go on, and then we'll see. Questioned - If it would be awakening to be a sleepwalker for a long time. - He answered. Maybe everything tomorrow. Questioned - If he wanted to wake up. - He answered. Yes, and so it was done.

Same day an hour later.
It was an opportunity for the magnetizer to meet and invite the Lords Dr. Xidian, and Mr. Martini

to be witnesses of the sleep produced by one chamber to another with the intermediate of a wall - Mr. Mustoxidi joined them. , and the effect was the usual, although the Zerboni could not know the return of it magnetizer not that the experiment to which it was subjected - the sleep was produced in two minutes - manifested that it was, unnecessarily they called it several times the Lords Martini and Mustoxidi, while at the magnetizer he answered immediately when he spoke in a low voice - The infirm showed a rather frowning of this compulsion to a new sleep. Questioned if he could still be magnetized for many days. - Responds. Until 8:30 am tomorrow morning for at that hour I have to break that thread that holds the lung attached - then I will have to suffer a severe pain, and as soon as the thread is broken I wil wake up for myself. When questioned whether from then on he could exercise on her any magnetic action. - Responds. None. At his request he was woken up.

Day 21 July around 8 o'clock.

The Lords Doctor Semo, Braila, Lavrano, Lessi, Professor Orioli and others intervened. Without previous precaution of the patient, magnetic sleep was induced in two minutes by magnetizing it from the other room. - First she sat on the bed, and she fell down stretched out - Called then by several bystanders did not answer them - Entered the magnetizer, to corresponding queries with her, gave an answer - That was better very - and saw more obscurely than in the day He made her rise so sleepy, and leading her by hand he led her into the bedroom where he had magnetized her, and made her lie down in another bed - Precisely here he guessed the hour that was - Immediately after commencing with ... unknown to her, and asked her if she saw any illness in them - although she reluctantly even won by repeated requests, swiping her hand from head to foot on the counselor, she said - This young man must have suffered an impure business disease with a woman (so he was confessed); and he then pointed out exactly the places of pain; and he added that the mercurial frictions were necessary: nevertheless, they would have done little, since the evil was too old. Removed this first consultant - and replaced him Mr. Doctor Lavrana, he recognized - That he had no illness: he said more - You are a doctor, and you can know your state better than me. When questioned, the infirm questioned how much time the thread was missing - he answered. Fifteen minutes. Questioned if he saw clearly. - He answered. That his internal sight became on the contrary ever more obscure, and that if there still remained some ray of light, this came from the intense action that the magnetizer exercised on the forehead and on the stomach. A few minutes later this and other answers, he began to have convulsive fluttering and to gasp - He was calmed by reinforcing the magnetic action with a more energetic will. Asked then as he felt - He replied after two minutes of silence -

Oh, it's better but the thread is not broken yet - And here, in a very short interval, returns to anguish more than before, the chest rises. Breathing becomes excessively short and frequent. Send moans that gradually increase until they become loud cries - Then he says - Now it breaks - it seems that a hand will fall over it and cut the thread - In fact after a very strong scream woke up all happy, nothing remembering that ch ' had been, showing herself surprised to find herself in a different room from the one she had been before, and complaining about the prank that she supposed she had been made by her companions - She is fine. In the afternoon hours of the same day, and in the following days, we tried in vain to go back to producing magnetic sleep, or at least some sensible effect - the convulsive shocks to which it was subjected are no longer renewed. She is healthy.

Chapter 10 - True astrology

In this chapter we will briefly discuss the real foundations for the study and development of an astrology based on valid principles. For centuries now the understanding of these laws on which the true astrology was based has been lost, and what remains today is nothing but a pile of rubble in the hands of charlatans who exploit the ignorance and ingenuity of others. The bases of astrology, that is, of the science that holds the planets responsible for certain influences on organic life and to a greater extent on the human being, are based primarily on the law of sects. Through the law of the seven we learn that organic life was created precisely to bridge the gap between the planets of the solar system and the Earth. The law of the seven shows us that the radiations of the planets can not reach the Earth because they are between the interval FA - MI, and without an additional help I can not be absorbed by the Earth. The medium that provides this shock is organic life. In this case, organic life is provided with greater sensitivity and succeeds, therefore, in absorbing the planetary radiations so transformed can be transmitted to the Earth. In this way the interval between FA and MI is filled and the eighth descending radiation can continue without problems. The influences of the planets on organic life are already demonstrated by the law of sects. In other words, it is the same law of the seven that indicates that these influences exist without any doubt. Once you understand this, it remains to be seen how these influences act on organic life and especially on human beings. The capital error of ordinary astrology is the belief that these influences are visibly manifest to anyone's eyes and can easily be classified and inferred based on correspondences with the zodiacal signs. Nothing could be further from reality. According to the absurdities of this pseudo-astrology, the results of planetary influences are specific personality traits in a given subject born under a specific zodiacal sign. We will not speak now of the ignorance of ordinary astrology on the astronomical phenomenon called "precession of the equinoxes", which in our era determines a displacement of a zodiacal sign back, so much so that today at the Spring equinox is not the constellation of Aries as a background to the rising Sun but that of Pisces. Because of this, everyone should actually move a sign back from the zodiacal sign that is attributed to them by astrology to obtain the actual corresponding sign, that is, the real constellation that was the background to the rising of the Sun on the day of his birth. In this chapter we will not even talk about the single and real influence that each planet has taken singularly, which does not correspond at all with what ordinary astrology affirms, since what is really understood at the beginning is that all the results of planetary influences are not visible through manifestations and personality traits, as is generally believed in astrology, but they act and lie in the subconscious. Personality originates from the influences of the environment and not, as is mistakenly believed, by planetary influences. Personality is artificial, it is that which does not belong to man, while the essence is the real man. For this reason, the same planetary influences can only be seen by those who have succeeded in the task of separating the essence from the personality, after a long and serious inner work. The essence becomes subconscious due to the formation and dominance that acquires the personality that has formed in complete contrast to the essence and which acts as a crust. The reason why anyone who has encountered considerable difficulty in trying to distinguish the essence from the personality lies in the fact that the essence is subconscious and therefore imperceptible in the ordinary state in which man finds himself. Those who believe it is possible to study the influence of the planets without first making the subconscious conscious. We have already talked about the error of considering "conscious" what consciously has nothing and what else is nothing but the whole of the automatic functioning of the personality, since both its formation and its subsequent manifestations are absolutely unconscious. In addition to determining the essence of man, planetary influences also produce effects in the body. For example, it is very probable that the full Moon causes motor changes through an initial amplification of the spinal reflexes followed by their weakening and increases the electrical activity of dopaminergic neurons,

Chapter 11 - The influence of the planets on the human body

The following is my translation from the Latin of Mesmer's thesis, entitled "Dissertatio physico-medica de planetarum influxu" (Wien, 1766).

Since ancient times there has been the habit of mortals to observe and recognize the influence of the planets; as in agriculture, in the nautical art and in medicine that attributed this power to them, until the astrologers came up, who with their innumerable and absurd falsities corrupted this truth and deformed it. However, recently the philosophers engaged in gloriously eradicating the prejudices of the past, annihilated the rumors so completely superstitious of the astrologers, but largely remained the senseless justification of the suburbs of the people. Then came the great Newton, who told the truth about the geometric laws followed by nature, inspired our own contemplation of the fabric of the world and the laws of attraction, from which the universe is governed. Although the illustrious men have always been on the path of the knowledge of attraction, Newton deserves the highest praise because he illustrated it to the best, with multiple experiments and observations, so he mostly turned to the interpretation of the phenomena of the sky. We look at the system without a doubt with the reason for accommodating experiences for our purpose. All bodies are directed in the same way, or tend to the same direction by force, each of the individual particles of matter adapts, it follows that the body is moved differently from all the joint forces of the particles, from which the body is format; therefore this force grows in time, in the moment in which the quantity of matter increases, and it is immutable in the single particles, at the same distance always equal, while at a great distance it diminishes, as it is increased by the square of distance. To this phenomenon that goes and that comes has been given the name of Gravity or Attraction, and is ascribed in the universal law of nature. All bodies are in the same gravity. At different distances it is inverse according to the square. In reality this gravity has been assigned to the system of our planet, has been demonstrated by the phenomena. The planets, with the movement of the first distances from the different distances from the sun and in the same way from the ratio of the masses, are brought close to the system of all bodies to the approach belonging to the center of gravity, which together with the great power of the sun, which it is not far from the same, far above the remaining bodies. Their movements take place in elliptical orbits. The orbits are established by each of the major planets, so one of the fires falls in the center of the sun, so that a planet comes to the sun and in the same way moves away. The distance varies from the focus to the center of the particles, and depends on the speed and direction of the first distances, the greater the retreat, the closer it is to the sun. The planets do not move at the same speed in all points of their orbits, which is less than the sun, so it moves faster. Squares are the times of the single periods of the orbits, so the maximum diameters of the cube. These laws of sky motion discovered by Kepler are prior to the subsequent observations validated by astronomers. Therefore the phenomenon of motion belongs to the masses, which therefore on both sides are moved, as they are kept in their orbit by the forces existing in the fire, it is shown by the mathematicians and the astronomers, so they are alternatively driven by one another: in fact in each mass, which is moved according to a curved line, there are two remarkable active forces alternately, of which, on the one hand one retains the mass with a curvilinear wake, on the other, in the same way, pushes it forward towards some point of the center. At the same time these curvilinear motion is produced by these agents. Thus the force is produced, which attracts the planets to the sun. Moreover, whenever the opposite action is always the same, it is the inevitable reaction: the sun is attracted to the same planets, and furthermore, from the single rule, which is among them, it is deduced that the mass of these is subjected to the antagonistic motion of the Sun. Although they are propelled by a light motion, the orbits of the planets are delineated, and this movement of the sun is confirmed by observations. When in the common motion they revolve around the sun, however, the force from which these are pushed to the sun is clear, and they push those in the same movement. The astronomers observed to divert a bit 'the trajectory of Saturn when Jupiter was closer to the planet: in this way, as the observations agree that Jupiter and Saturn are mutually loaded. No doubt it is derived from the calculation of the movements, which these are produced by the law of attraction. The gravity of Mars in the sun is decreased by 1/12512 by the action of Jupiter. Moreover from the reciprocal action of the planets it follows that they are transported in weak elliptical orbits. From the Flamstedio observation, Saturn upsets the motion of Jupiter's satellites, attracts these a little. The motion of the comets also depends on the law of gravity, and this is revealed by the observations, and in view of this, around the planets, the gravity of the sun prevails, and from this trail regulated by gravity are deviated. But the curve of the direction depends in the same way also on this gravity, so the body traces an ellipse, or rather a parabola, a hyperbole, in whose fire there is the sun. Although the calculation of the Moon is off target of its action, however, it is essential to evaluate and briefly expose the mutual gravity of the Earth and the Moon, and that these phenomena are related to the sun, so it is easy to understand the general energy of the forces. Furthermore,

The Moon travels an elliptical orbit around the Earth. Therefore, from the considered motion of the Moon and from the approach of the Sun, the gravity of the Moon on Earth is reduced; and at the same time, when it is less attracted by the Earth, it moves further away from it, and in its departure a diminution of this gravity is produced, which is strengthened in this case by the distance of the Moon. Thus, considering the motion of the phenomena that result from the attraction of the Moon, for the same cause occur the changes on the Earth, which occur with the effect of the tides. Therefore, this influence of the Moon is manifest. Moreover, in another way it is the quality of the influence on the animal body, which is not judged to depend on the common qualities; but rather by the same force, which upsets the surface of the heavens with secretions, which influences the innermost part of matter, immense spheres in its orbit retains, separates from the passage in various situations, upsets, which is the cause of this universal gravity, and which is the probable principle of all the properties of bodies; in fact, in the particles of the minimum fluid parts and of the solid parts of our machine (of our body), it tends, relaxes, agitates: cohesion, elasticity, irritability, magnetism, electricity; and then, with good reason, it can be called animal gravity. The influences on our body derive from the motion of the larger bodies, which accurately bring order into the bodies. The insistence is characterized by the luminous matter, however the effectiveness of this is unknown in changing the animal body. A minimal part concerns the whole system of the nerves which in the human body is exposed to receive the pressures of the luminous matter of the day, a matter endowed with the force necessary to disturb it entirely and to provoke extraordinary changes in the body and mind. Now that we establish the existence of this influence that insinuates itself in all parts of the body and in its structure, in the senses of all the nerves, and acts on the same fluid of the nerves, whoever is surprised, if any of its alterations afflict the whole structure? Therefore, with this consideration, no paradox appears, if we declare that disturbances occur in the human body, due to the same forces acting on the atmosphere and the sea, and that our moods have varied differently according to the organs involved, and then upset, uplifted, producing an abundant turning in the head. In plants there is an elevated lymph during the full moon. The same is shown in the knowledge of diseases: epileptic seizures are used mainly in periods of full moon, hence the name of lunatic disease. Galen states: "The Moon commands epileptic periods". The sailor Thom Londini, accused the moon new and full for the manifestation of his illness. From Bartolin: an epileptic girl had her face surrounded by patches, which due to the various phases of the moon made the appearance varied. Therefore the singular case examined by Kerckring is worthy of mention. The ladies, who at the time of the full moon had a round face and no doubt beautiful, also with the Moon decreasing, the eyes, the nose and mouth turned to one side, so that they looked so deformed that they did not have the courage to present themselves in public, until with the crescent Moon it did not return to normalize the beauty of their appearance again. The states of hysteria and hypochondria are controlled by the influence of the moon. Doctors have experienced vertigo, paralysis, and often trembling. They are found among the common people delirious madness that fall into the periodic cycle of the Moon. It is not a vain supposition that the menstruation of women is caused by the Moon, moreover the elderly from assiduous observation declare that the purges, certainly, according to this rule, chase periodically in all the females unless they are infusing these inconstant influences of the celestial body, the nourishment of each and the lifestyle, the distinction of infinite combinations, and the strength of most uncertain circumstances and power, increases because in the areas closest to the equator, where we show the influence of the moon being stronger, we they produce abundant menstrual flows, while they are reduced by this, where it approaches the proportion of the Poles. For the same cause, bleeding also occurs during the period of the influences. It was observed by Musgravio, the case of a young man spitting blood for the middle of the year, when the new moon recurred regularly. At a certain host in winter, from the age of 43 to 55, he periodically chased a blood spill from the index finger of his right hand, almost every month, and always in the full moon, just before the next arrival of the equinox. It is not to forget the experience of Sanctorio, because he taught us that the healthy bodies of the males and with a very balanced lifestyle, no doubt they usually become heavier in a particular period of the months, weighing two pounds, and are reduced to the usual weight about towards the end of the month becoming similar to that of women, and that moreover is caused a period of urine a little 'more abundant and cloudy. Baglivi talks about some men suffering from fistula in the intestine, which used to secrete a large amount of faeces with the crescent moon and which at the same time dwindled with the decreasing Moon; Mead associated the story of an adolescent, who at every full moon, because of venereal disease, provoked an ulceration, screeched in pain, the continuous flow stopped after a week, and always during the full moon it reappeared spontaneously. Tulpio observed pains in the kidneys coming and going during the lunar period. Helmontio and Floyero observed that they suffered from respiratory failure with a monthly recurrence. Galen deduced that type of acute illness in which the effectiveness of the Moon is manifested on the seventh day, the fourteenth and the twenty first. Epidemic states of the years deserve to be reported.

The skilled Sidenamo who recognized the uncommon disease from other fevers; no doubt he somehow observed the age in which it manifests itself, in what season they clearly corresponded, in a very different way a multitude of men were infested and because of these exterminated. The various conditions, of heat, of cold, of dryness, of humidity, also depended on some rather occult alteration in the depths of the earth itself, from which the air is contaminated by its outflows, from which human bodies to this or that disease they are condemned. It is evident from the predominance of the pre-announced conditions, which are precisely exerted by the perfect orbit, and therefore change to another location. They further explained these facts, which Cl wrote. Ramazzin. In the city, and in the Modena countryside, among those peoples, for years in succession a very dangerous fever raged, and it was observed, he said, that after the full moon, and with the moon much quieter, this fever acted with violence, and that later it attenuated with the new moon; not only that, but the observation also found other teachers agree, which contributed to the prognosis and treatment of these fevers. No doubt it was surprising what happened on January 21, 1693. There was a lunar eclipse during the night. A complete lunar eclipse most of the diseases disappeared, and at the same time, while this lunar eclipse occurred, some men suddenly died. The story of a certain Belloni was also very appropriate; states: some doctors, they reflected on the manifest health of some women,

And everyone was surprised to see that it had not returned before him, after the splendor of light had returned to heaven.

Diemerbroekuis carefully established the nature and progress of the new and full moon's influence. Countless testimonies and observations show how the Moon and the Sun act on the physical strength of men, unfortunately the doctors from too early judgment have long condemned this truth; the truth, which rightly had been evaluated, subsequently due to certain convictions in the natural sciences and medicine, was later abandoned. Furthermore, we hypothesize that the universal energy on us of celestial bodies is not limited to illnesses alone.

It is amazing the harmony that exists between these bodies, and the power of the ineffable universal gravity on our bodies that are attracted in harmony and not all equally in the same way; therefore, as a musical instrument is provided by several strings, absolutely a certain tone resounds, whereby, in some place it is emanated in a uniform way, so in the same way that the bodies are agitated by sex, age, all balance, and the individual arrangements are established, and possess a certain harmony accorded by the position of the stars. Later, although this supposition of destiny that originates from planetary influences was rejected, as it troubled the minds of physicians, it was evident that natural law manifested itself, upsetting the harmonious order of the human body, and was able to change,

I believe there is an influence that shakes the human bodies that are strongly disturbed by the celestial bodies because of the multiplicity of their movements and subjected to the contrary influences; how correct, useful and complete advice is it to ask physicians to observe this influence of celestial bodies carefully and with little concern at all? For this reason, I consider it appropriate to bring to light a great deal of medical knowledge, and find ways to increase the full willingness of the doctors.

Chapter 12 - Ashyata Sheyimash: a real character unknown to historians

On the important figure of Ashyata Sheyimash, presented by Gurdjieff in his work "The Tales of Beelzebub to his nephew", three types of incorrect interpretations have developed and spread. Some have wanted to see the figure of Gurdjieff himself, others have tried to make it coincide with some well-known characters in history and still others have committed the usual mistake of interpreting allegorically what instead should be taken literally. If it were some character already known to our history, Gurdjieff would have openly cited it as when he talks about Pythagoras, Leonardo da Vinci, Mesmer and many others. In this case, Ashyata Sheyimash is a historical figure that really existed, but of which our historians of all ages know nothing. D ' on the other hand, Gurdjieff himself explains the reasons for this historical ignorance, clearly stating that Ashyata Sheyimash has fallen into historical oblivion because of the fact that he preferred not to publicly and openly teach ordinary people as they did, for example, Jesus, Buddha and many others. , but he did his work by preparing some initiated beings who were later sent to teach other people. Gurdjieff provides a wealth of accurate information regarding Ashyata Sheyimash. He was born in a village near Babylon exactly 700 years before the Babylonian events. The Babylonian events reported by Gurdjieff took place at the time of Cambyses II of Persia who conquered Egypt in 525 BC, after which many scholars, among whom was also Pythagoras, were brought to Babylon. Then, carefully following the indications of Gurdjieff, we know that Ashyata Sheyimash was born in a village near Babylon in about 1225 BC. In the subsequent work entitled "Encounters with Extraordinary Men", Gurdjieff states that the brotherhood of the Essenes was founded one thousand two hundred years before the birth of Christ, thus in the same period in which the action of Master Ashyata Sheyimash took place. I have no doubt that the founding of the brotherhood of the Essenes, in which Jesus received his first teachings twelve hundred years later, was determined by the work of Ashyata Sheyimash. Another noteworthy thing is that Ashyata Sheyimash was the only one sent from above to be able to settle things on the earth, even for about 200 years, while others like Buddha, Jesus, Muhammad, etc., they failed for several reasons. After the efforts of Ashyata Sheyimash, a period of peace finally reigned on the earth and all kings and emperors became such, no longer on the basis of what I call "artificial hierarchy" founded on selfishness and the unconsciousness of man, but on the basis of the "natural hierarchy" determined by the degree of reason and being reached by certain conscious individuals. It is probable that King

Solomon was one of the last kings of this period of splendor, the fruit of Ashyata Sheyimash's labors. "The stories of Beelzebub to his nephew" has 3 reading plans. The first literal, the second analogical and the third allegorical. It is the masterpiece of a superior mind. The three floors overlap harmoniously without the one excluding the more, just like a cosmos that contains another. On the allegorical plane, in some precise points, the literal plane is superimposed, without the one excluding the other. In other precise points, the literal plane is superimposed on the analogical plane, always without the one excluding the other. Only the allegorical plane is omnipresent in the work, while the other two planes alternate and intertwine with allegory as in a sacred dance. Gurdjieff had said that the horns of the animals depicted in some French caves he had visited along with some of his pupils represented varying degrees of human evolution, just like the horns of Beelzebub. Gurdjieff also reports that the

Sarmung school was founded in 2500 BC in Babylon and, from my point of view, the true scholars among which Pythagoras was also found, gathered in Babylon around 500 BC, to find the solution so that the great knowledge was preserved to future generations, that is the "adherents to the legamonismo", were part of this esoteric school that in full period of the "Soliunensius" process, they were working hard to gather and preserve the great knowledge. In the book "Fragments of an Unknown Teaching", Gurdjieff speaks openly about this collection and preservation of the great knowledge of some conscious individuals that always coincides with the periods in which the revolutions occur, the great wars, the natural cataclysms, and a whole series of destructive events in which the great knowledge is likely to be lost. A king is a slave to his servants, as are his servants. It is a universal principle that manifests itself whenever it refers to the "artificial hierarchies" created by man. Conversely, there is a "natural hierarchy" that is dictated by the degree of being achieved, and there, who is above, is free and its authority is not a factor of slavery for those under it, rather, it is a possibility of liberation. We must never confuse the artificial hierarchy with the natural one, and never forget that the creators and supporters of the artificial hierarchy in their adherence to this structure, which as demonstrated leads to mutual slavery, then to pure mutual loss, show all their lack of understanding of great knowledge. In a world where the system of mutual support is based on the exploitation of man by man, a high position on the social scale must necessarily correspond to a greater degree of parasitism. In such a system, a kitchen-boy is countless times less parasitic than a holder of power, such as a King, a Prince, a President, or a leader of any kind. The ordinary conception, therefore, to consider the one who does not work the parasite par excellence, is totally devoid of logic. or a leader of any kind. The ordinary conception, therefore, to consider the one who does not work the parasite par excellence, is totally devoid of logic. or a leader of any kind. The ordinary conception, therefore, to consider the one who does not work the parasite par excellence, is totally devoid of logic.

Chapter 13 - The Bukharian Dervish Hadji-Assvatz-Truv and the Objective Music

In the third book of the work "The Tales of Beelzebub to his nephew", the first chapter is dedicated to communicating to the reader the important historical data concerning the discovery of the law of sects and the events that led to the forgetting of this fundamental law. These historical events that really happened in the remote past of our planet were certainly learned by Gurdjieff through his intense research, and almost certainly were communicated by that small group of individuals who had kept this knowledge through the millennia up to our days, probably by members of the Sarmoung fraternity. The chapter in question is titled "Beelzebub tells how men have known and forgotten the fundamental cosmic law of Heptaparaparshinokh". Through this chapter we learn that this law was first discovered on the continent Atlantis by Theophanus, one of the members of the Atlantean scientific society called Akhaldan. After the sinking of the continent of Atlantis, this knowledge was lost and Gurdjieff hypothesizes that in this historical period no ties were created because most probably this knowledge was so widespread that they did not consider it necessary to take any precaution to ensure that it was not lost in course of successive generations.

It is necessary to understand that the sinking of Atlantis was caused by the fact that the center of gravity of the planet Earth was completely unbalanced after the impact of the comet in the Pacific Ocean that gave rise to the two moons. In this way a huge gash was created in the Pacific, still present, while the force of this impact transmitting up to the opposite side of the planet caused the continent Atlantis to rise from the seabed, whose composition was surely of basalt, typical composition of the crust oceanic and different from the normal continental crust, which means much heavier, since the density of the basalt is greater than the composition of the continental crust. Imagine now the full extent of the imbalance of the earth's center of gravity. On one side an immense gash (the pacific ocean), while on the opposite side there is a vast protrusion of dense and heavy basalt rising from the seabed of the Atlantic ocean and that was to form the continent of Atlantis. Since its inception, Atlantis had to have the days counted. After this catastrophe many acquaintances were lost and with them the knowledge of the law of sects, called Heptaparaparshinokh. Centuries passed before it was rediscovered this time by two Chinese scholars. I find it superfluous to dwell further on this subject, since everyone can learn the rest of the information from the chapter in question. Rather, let us briefly pass to the next chapter, which is the second chapter of the third book. This chapter is titled "The Bukharian Dervish Hadji-Assvatz-Truv" and Gurdjieff through the character of Beelzebub tells us about his own experiences in this period of his life. Traces of this period and of these experiences of Gurdjieff are also found in the book "Meetings with extraordinary men", in the second sub-chapter called "Solov'ëv" which is part of the chapter dedicated to Prince Jurij Ljubovedskij, on page 192 of the Adelphi edition.

It is easy to understand that it is the same Hadji-Zefir-Boga-Eddin, of which Gurdjieff / Beelzebub speaks in the second chapter of the third book. Needless to say that Gurdjieff provides unknown historical data along with those already well known and this because on one hand his personal research was conducted in a very thorough and on the other because he knew the few individuals who had kept them from the remote past to the days our. So much so that we know nothing of Zebek, while Charles Cagniard de Latour, we know that he was born in 1777 and died in 1859, and we know what were his most important inventions, including the siren usable as an instrument for measuring the acoustic frequencies . And again, when the Bukharian dervish Hadji-Assvatz-Truv, describes the death of his friend, it 's easy even to understand in what period it happened, and this to demonstrate once again that Gurdjieff is presenting, on the one hand his real experiences lived in first person and on the other hand the important events happened in the past of our planet of which the historians ancient and modern know nothing at all. The death of the friend of the Bukharian dervish Hadji-Assvatz-Truv took place during the period of the first Anglo-Afghan war, ie between 1839 and 1842. So much so that Gurdjieff when he meets this dervish, he is already old as he himself says ; and presumably this meeting took place between the late nineteenth and early twentieth centuries. You do not need to go any further, as anyone can read these chapters in person and learn as much as possible.

Chapter 14 - A story about Gurdjieff's "inner consideration"

Once upon a time there was a couple with a 12 year old son and a donkey. They decided to travel, work and learn about the world. So they all left with their donkey. Arrived in the first country, people commented: "Look at that boy how rude ... he is on the donkey and the poor parents, already elderly, who pull him." Then the wife said to her husband: "We do not allow people to talk badly about our son." The husband took him down and climbed onto the donkey. Arrived at the second country, people murmured: "Look how shameful that guy ... let the boy and the poor wife pull the ass while he is comfortably on his back." Then, they made the decision to pick up his wife , while father and son held the reins to pull the donkey. Arrived at the third country, people commented: "Poor man! after having worked all day, let his wife get on the donkey ... and poor son ... who knows what's up to him, with a mother like that! and they decided to sit down all three on the donkey to begin the pilgrimage again.We arrived at the next village, they listened to what the people of the village said: "They are beasts, more beasts of the donkey that carries them ... they will split their backs! In the end, they decided to go down and walk together with the donkey but, passing through the next village, they could not believe what the voices said laughing: "Look at those three idiots, they walk, even if they have a donkey that could bring them!" . and poor son ... who knows what's up to him, with a mother like that! Then they agreed and decided to sit down all three on the donkey to begin the pilgrimage again. Arrived at the next village, they listened to what the people of the village said: "They are beasts, more beasts of the donkey that brings them ... they will break their backs! In the end, they decided to get off everyone and walk with the donkey but, passing for the next country, they could not believe what the voices were saying, laughing: "Look at those three idiots; they walk, even if they have a donkey that could bring them! " and poor son ... who knows what's up to him, with a mother like that! Then they agreed and decided to sit down all three on the donkey to begin the pilgrimage again. Arrived at the next village, they listened to what the people of the village said: "They are beasts, more beasts of the donkey that brings them ... they will break their backs! In the end, they decided to get off everyone and walk with the donkey but, passing for the next country, they could not believe what the voices were saying, laughing: "Look at those three idiots; they walk, even if they have a donkey that could bring them! " they listened to what the people of the village said: "They are beasts, more beasts of the donkey that carries them ... they will break their backs!" In the end, they decided to get off and walk together with the donkey but, passing through the next village, they could not believe what the voices were saying, laughing: "Look at those three idiots; they walk, even if they have a donkey that could bring them! " they listened to what the people of the village said: "They are beasts, more beasts of the donkey that carries them ... they will break their backs!" In the end, they decided to get off and walk together with the donkey but, passing through the next village, they could not believe what the voices were saying, laughing: "Look at those three idiots; they walk, even if they have a donkey that could bring them! "

Chapter 15 - Okidanokh, periodic table and the three balanced brains

In the universe everything is one, even matter. Matter and energy are also one, they are two aspects of one and the same phenomenon. All chemical elements, molecules, electromagnetism, electricity, magnetism, etc., are nothing but modifications of one and the same material called eternalkrilno. The engine of all modifications of eternalkrilno is a very particular matter called okidanokh. The okidanokh is the first matter to be formed in the universe, at the moment when the emanations of the Absolute Sun meet eternalkrilno. The okidanokh is the subtlest material in the universe, for this reason it is present everywhere and penetrates everything, in other words it is omnipresent, omnipresent and omnipetering. The Absolute Sun is an astronomical body around which all galaxies rotate; it is the physical brain and the mind of God, the supreme intelligence. Outside the Absolute Sun there is an inert and primordial material called eternokrilno. The eternalkrilno is the primordial matter that forms the basis of all that exists and glues between the various distinct parts that constitute any existing concentration. The okidanokh material has unique properties that no other material possesses. Electricity, electromagnetism and artificial light are all produced by the mutual union or destruction of two parts of the kokanoan. The okidanokh matter is formed, according to the law of the trinity, by three independent and opposing forces: the active force, the passive force and the neutralizing force. Every existing matter, therefore, contains in itself all three forces, only that the proportions between these forces is different. All the modifications produced between their proportions, cause the transformation of a matter into another more subtle or coarser. With an increase in the active strength of the kokidanokh, the proportions are modified, and a given matter is transmuted into a subtler matter.

To an increase of the passive strength dell'okidanokh, the subject undergoes an involution and becomes coarser. The difference in electrical potential is caused by one of the peculiarities of the ukidanokh, namely the tendency to form a single whole when the parts are momentarily separated or disproportionate. The radiations that our Sun produces are the third force resulting from the meeting of two parts of the Akidanokh, one active and the other passive. All the existing phenomena are produced by the characteristics of the kokanoan, especially those that occur in the atmosphere of the planets. The ionization of the terrestrial ionosphere caused by the radiations of the Sun, is the manifestation of another characteristic dell'okidanokh. The subject that takes the name of "amber" it is constituted by identical proportions of the three separate forces of the kokanoan, for this reason the amber is an insulator with respect to the three separate flows of the three forces that would otherwise alter the proportions. All the properties of the chemical elements of the periodic table are dictated by the proportions of these three forces. The electronegative elements are characterized by a predominant mass of the passive strength of the kokanoan. On the contrary, the "electropositive" elements have a predominant mass of the active force. It is precisely this difference in proportions that causes the attraction between these two kinds of elements that tend to unite in a single whole to achieve a certain equilibrium between the proportions of the three separate forces of the ukidanokh. Fluorine that possesses 9 protons (active force), 10 neutrons (neutralizing force) and 10 electrons (passive force), with a prevalence in the proportions of the neutralizing and passive force, tends to join, for example, with lithium which has a number of 3 protons, 4 neutrons and 2 electrons. In forming the lithium fluoride, the proportions between the active force and the passive force reach equilibrium, in fact the lithium fluoride has a number of protons equal to 12, and a number of electrons equal to 12. These are the proportions of the three separate parts dell'okidanokh to cause attraction. The noble gases are constituted by balanced proportions of the three forces of the Akidanokh, for this reason they are non-reactive. Helium, for example, is made up of 2 protons, 2 neutrons and 2 electrons, and the neon of 10 protons, 10 neutrons and 10 electrons, and this is true of all other noble gases. With regard to this, it is interesting to note that the properties of the law of the three are universal. Just as noble gases, constituted by balanced proportions of the three forces of the Akidanokh, do not react to external forces, in the same way a human being who has the three balanced brains, whose formation always originates from the three forces of the Akidanokh, not reacts like an automaton under the force of forces coming from the environment. Originally, the sphinx's head had the form of two breasts of a virgin depicting love, and th's head had been separated from the trunk by means of amber to indicate that love had to be impartial and not influenced by all the rest. A true symbol of conscious love. Once again I have shown that in the work "The Tales of Beelzebub to his nephew" the only allegory present is constituted by the three main characters that run throughout the work, ie Beelzebub, Hassin and Ahun, whose meaning has been explained in previous articles. When we become aware of how a principle of the law of the three can manifest itself equally in totally different phenomena, what are the noble gases of the periodic table and the human being who has attained the state of "all balanced brains", we realize that these parts of Gurdjieff's work concern the principle of analogy and do not represent any allegory. To do this, Gurdjieff must necessarily deal with scientific topics, and who can understand, he will see the marvelous analogies that manifest themselves between distinct phenomena, which are the clear universality of the laws explained. In speaking literally about matter, about its secrets, about the secrets of the universe, Gurdjieff wants to show us that the same results that conform to the laws that are produced in nature are produced at the same time in us. Man is a miniature universe, created in the precise image of the great universe. Every matter, substance, element, etc., occupy a precise plane in the universe and carry out precise functions, therefore, given the precise analogy between man and the universe, it is possible to know one from the study of the other, however, it remains the importance of the degree of being in relation to the knowledge that produces understanding. Allegorically interpret the parts of the work that deals with the principles of objective science, means not having understood anything. In showing us that the Suns of the universe correspond to our organic parts, Gurdjieff is telling us: "As above, so below". When Gurdjieff speaks of the suns, of the two moons, dell'okidanokh, when he refers to historical data, it must be taken absolutely literally. The key in these cases is not the allegory, but the analogy, the motto "as above, so below." In the work there is also an allegorical part, and is that made up of the three main characters, This allegory has 7 meanings that we have already explained in a previous chapter: Do you still remember that understanding is the result of the development of being in relation to knowledge? In showing us that the Suns of the universe correspond to our organic parts, Gurdjieff is telling us: "As above, so below". When Gurdjieff speaks of the suns, of the two moons, dell'okidanokh, when he refers to historical data, it must be taken absolutely literally. The key in these cases is not the allegory, but the analogy, the motto "as above, so below." In the work there is also an allegorical part, and is that made up of the three main characters, This allegory has 7 meanings that we have already explained in a previous chapter: Do you still remember that understanding is the result of the development of being in relation to knowledge? In showing us that the Suns of the universe correspond to our organic parts, Gurdjieff is telling us: "As above, so below". When Gurdjieff speaks of the suns, of the two moons, dell'okidanokh, when he refers to historical data, it must be taken absolutely literally. The key in these cases is not the allegory, but the analogy, the motto "as above, so below." In the work there is also an allegorical part, and is that made up of the three main characters, This allegory has 7 meanings that we have already explained in a previous chapter: Do you still remember that understanding is the result of the development of being in relation to knowledge? When Gurdjieff speaks of the suns, of the two moons, dell'okidanokh, when he refers to historical data, it must be taken absolutely literally. The key in these cases is not the allegory, but the analogy, the motto "as above, so below." In the work there is also an allegorical part, and is that made up of the three main characters, This allegory has 7 meanings that we have already explained in a previous chapter: Do you still remember that understanding is the result of the development of being in relation to knowledge? When Gurdjieff speaks of the suns, of the two moons, dell'okidanokh, when he refers to historical data, it must be taken absolutely literally. The key in these cases is not the allegory, but the analogy, the motto "as above, so below." In the work there is a so an allegorical part, and is that made up of the three main characters, This allegory has 7 meanings that we have already explained in a previous chapter: Do you still remember that understanding is the result of the development of being in relation to knowledge? and it is that constituted by the three main characters, This allegory has 7 meanings that we have already explained in a previous chapter. Do you still remember that understanding is the result of the development of being in relation to knowledge? and it is that constituted by the three main characters, This allegory has 7 meanings that we have already explained in a previous chapter. Do you still remember that understanding is the result of the development of being in relation to knowledge?

The last curiosity I want to highlight, without affirming anything absolute about it, is that which follows. The old spaceships described by Gurdjieff used a propulsion that exploited the elekilpomagtistion, in other words the electromagnetism, which is the result, or the third force, which is produced by the meeting of two parts of the Akidanokh, an active part other passive. The most authoritative hypotheses on the propulsive system of UFOs, which are based on some characteristics observed in the sightings present in the UFO case studies, affirm that most probably it is an application unknown to us of electromagnetism.

Chapter 16 - On the differences between Ouspensky and Gurdjieff

The purpose of this chapter is to help neutralize, as much as possible, the problems that some encounter when they compare the teaching of Gurdjieff transmitted by Ouspensky through his book "Fragments of an Unknown Teaching", which is a true testimony of a student's experience, and the exact same teaching in the form given to him by Gurdjieff through the written works of his own hand. First of all, it must be emphasized that there are no differences in the essence of teaching, but only between the form and the terminology used by Gurdjieff in the period when Ouspensky was his pupil and the one present in the work "The stories of Beelzebub to his nephew. ". IS' It is also essential to point out that these difficulties arise in those who have faced all these ideas in opposition to the fundamental principles themselves that constitute teaching. In other words, those who perceive differences between what Ouspensky has said and what Gurdjieff has written do not do any work on themselves, and merely analyze all information with the intellect alone.

Gurdjieff continually warned of an excess of theory. The essence of this teaching consists in recognizing that man is asleep, therefore, he can not be master of his inner world and therefore not even of all its manifestations. Hypnotic sleep is caused by the fact that the bonds between its three brains are broken. The three brains are three tools of knowledge. If you use only one, you will only see a third of what you can see. This is why everything will seem contradictory and disconnected. In comparing the content of Ouspensky's book with that found in Gurdjieff's book, some confuse perception with being conscious, claiming that there is no correspondence between the two expositions of teaching, in other words, they create a real tower of Babel. Perceiving and being conscious is not the same thing. You can have automatic perceptions and conscious perceptions. Conscious perceptions occur in the state of self-remembering, and the state of self-remembering corresponds to having all three brains connected to each other, in this way they participate simultaneously in receiving impressions, then in the moment of perception, and in the manifestations that they derive from it. Conscious perception is a simultaneous perception of the 3 brains in receiving impressions. Thus the automatic and the conscious manifestations derive from the same question, that is from the contemporary work of the centers. Perceiving indicates only the instant in which impressions are received, this act can be automatic, if it is conducted from only one center at a time, semi-conscious if conducted by two centers, or conscious if the three centers are linked together and then work simultaneously when the impressions are received. I will now provide some brief indications to show that the apparent differences in teaching lie only in form and in terminology, while the essence remains unchanged. Before doing so, I also add that in Gurdjieff's work many of the ideas in Ouspensky's book are deepened and expanded. In Gurdjieff's book we find, for example, the expression "voluntary contemplation", which is nothing but a state in which the links between the three centers are established, as we speak in "Frammenti" by Ouspensky. In the "Nunzio del bene venturo", Gurdjieff uses the expression "contemplation-transformed" to define that process of comparison of different impressions already recorded in different brains. As you can see, Gurdjieff speaks of "maintaining contact with their internal and separate centers", ie the link between the 3 centers. Then he goes on to say that of the three states consciousness the one considered higher for man comes from the associations produced by "contemplation-transformed", in other words it is the same thing that is reported by Ouspensky, namely the importance of the links between the three centers . And since "self-remembering" occurs when the 3 centers are connected, there is no difference between what Ouspensky reports in "Frammenti" and what Gurdjieff writes in his works. Others say that in the "Beelzebub" Gurdjieff does not talk about "bumpers" or "shock absorbers" reported instead by Ouspenky in "Frammenti", nothing more inaccurate. In fact, Gurdjieff talks about it constantly in the "Beelzebub", only that he calls them "self-tranquilizers". With regard to the first shock of "self-remembering" it is therefore obvious that when you "remember yourself", you are present when you receive impressions. The real state of "self-remembering" consists in establishing the link between the three centers that are generally disconnected. So much so that the state of hypnotic sleep, as we said, consists precisely in this disconnection between the centers. So, as it is easy to understand, we talk about the exact same thing. At this point it is easy to understand that the state of consciousness is the result obtained. If you remember yourself, you are present at the moment of receiving impressions, and this state is a state of consciousness opposed to not being present when you receive the impressions that will be called unconsciousness. There are no differences between what Ouspensky reports in "Frammenti" and what Gurdjieff writes in his works.

The differences are only in the terminology, in the form, the essence of the teaching is identical. The "bumpers" or "shock absorbers" are called "self-tranquilizers", the "link between the three centers" is called "contemplation-transformed" or "conscious contemplation", and so on. Having clarified this, now the really important question is that all these discussions of analysis and logic are opposed to the real work that Gurdjieff suggested. Again, Gurdjieff continually warned of the excess of theory. These operations of analysis are the automatic work of the intellectual center that elucubra taking the material from the "trainer", is the work of a single center, in other words, this excess in theorizing, is nothing but the work, however incorrect, of only one center, which is equivalent to a state of unconsciousness.

All the doubts that arise on the correctness of the theory can only be dissolved by practical experiments, just as in science all the hypotheses are confirmed or denied by the experiments. This teaching is also a tool to evaluate one's degree of being and one's level of understanding. If contradictions are found, or things that do not square, that is proof that understanding and being are at a low level. This awareness must push us to practical inner work. The only intellectual work, the sterile logic, the reasoning, do not correspond to the real inner work. Who has no conscience, looks for it in the definitions. Those who seek conscience in definitions, look for a corpse.

Chapter 17 - A key to understanding "Beelzebub's tales"

The work entitled "The Tales of Beelzebub to his nephew", written by Gurdjieff in the second half of the twentieth century, is based on three principles and has three levels of reading, all three fundamental. The first reading plan is the literal one which is based on the principle of the parallel development of knowledge and being from which comprehension arises. In view of this principle, since the development of knowledge and being influence each other, the reader is provided with a knowledge of the highest quality, which should not remain merely intellectual, otherwise, by failing at the same time a development of being, not there will be an increase in understanding. This reading plan, according to the law of the three, will be the passive force, that is the matter. The second level of reading is that of analogy which is based on the principle expressed by the formula "as above, so below". Based on this principle, Gurdjieff exposes the laws of objective science, the science of unity, the science of the whole. In this way it will be possible to observe that the results produced in a certain field by the fundamental laws are equally evident in all the other areas that have nothing in common between them. As we will see later, even the results produced by the laws in the periodic table of the elements are identical to those that occur in the human being. At this point, readers who will succeed by means of their conscious efforts to assimilate the essence of all this, will have developed in their emotional brain a feeling of the unity of everything. A person can know with his own intellect that there is a fundamental unity between all that exists, and to be in agreement or disagreement with this idea, but to feel this unity with one's own feeling radically changes everything. This second reading plan will represent the neutralizing force according to the law of the three. The third level of reading is based on the allegory, through which the science of being is exposed, whose principles show the possibilities that have been given to the human being in order to develop one's own being. This allegory is contained in the three main characters of the work, namely Beelzebub, his nephew Hassin and the faithful servant Ahun. This third plane of the work will be the active force of the sacred law of tri-unity. Unfortunately, many characters are contributing to distort the principles of teaching, some for commercial purposes, through books, conferences and courses, others because they are dominated by the weakness of wanting to appear wise, and still others for the simple reason of being without understanding. Thus we see rise to various absurdities about the "law of types", in which we try to define the principles using the theories of Jung that have no real value. The various manipulations that are undergoing the enneagram. The enneagram of personalities is another sad example of the degeneration that is affecting Gurdjieff's teaching, and so on. One of the most frequent errors is to maintain that the contents of the work "The Tales of Beelzebub to his Nephew" are only esoteric allegories. In reality, and on the other hand Gurdjieff himself declares it, in his work there is everything from the principles of objective science to the narration of important historical events unknown to us that have affected our planet. The only allegory present are the three characters who travel on the ship, namely Beelzebub, his nephew Hassin and the faithful servant Ahun. This allegory has seven precise meanings. The first makes us understand that in the moment in which reason has not yet reached a high degree, it can not live in a sphere in the cosmic order where the degree of reason is objectively high, in that the cosmic scales constitute a pyramid formed by different degrees of intelligence. In this scale of intelligence, the Sun, for example, is the most intelligent astronomical body in the solar system, immediately followed by the planet Jupiter, which is a Sun in the process of formation, and not as the current science holds it, a failed Sun. The places that make up the centers of the galaxies are more intelligent than the Suns, up to the supreme intelligence that is represented by the Absolute Sun, around which all the galaxies in the universe rotate. The Absolute Sun is an astronomical body, and it is both the physical brain and the mind of God. Notice how the classical contraposition between science and religion no longer has any raison d'etre. It originates from the very low degree of understanding of many human beings. On each cited astronomical body it is possible to live with a body adapted to that sphere of materials characterized by well-defined densities. The development of the degree of reason coincides with the formation of the corresponding subtle bodies. Just as it happens that on our plane of intelligence can be manifested beings that as to degree of reason belong to higher spheres, in the same way it can happen that in the high spheres a being arises whose reason is inferior to the degree required in that determined sphere . This is the case of the character used by Gurdjieff and called Beelzebub. Beelzebub (the immature reason) who lived on the Absolute Sun (a real astronomical body) thought illogical some things concerning the administration of the world, and to prevent it from erupting a revolution (disharmony), was sent into "exile" in the sphere suitable to its degree of reason (in the solar system, on the planet Mars) with the possibility of perfecting itself. At the time when Beelzebub is perfected (the objective mature reason) he can return to the high echelons of the cosmos. The second meaning illustrates how the perfected reason (Beelzebub) must instruct the feeling (Hassin), to allow it to develop and not remain in the infantile state, as is the case with the typical result obtained by Western education which is one-sided and too intellectual, and the passive role that must have, in all this, the faithful servant Ahun, that is the body. In general it happens that the ravenous instincts of the body direct the entire mechanical life of men; in the work of Gurdjieff, the faithful servant Ahun (the body) assists passive to the narratives of Beelzebub (perfected reason), and when Beelzebub pursues him, inviting him to say his own, in the chapter dedicated to Art, the faithful servant Ahun (the body) is expressed on the basis of perceptions conforming to his nature, that is by means of sensations, and in the attempt to imitate the typical way of expression of Beelzebub, shows another peculiar characteristic of the instinctive brain -motor, that is the tendency to imitation, its peculiar characteristic. The body must be the servant (the faithful servant Ahun) and not the master, as it happens in the life of most men. The third meaning of this allegory is a real manual on the psychology of children's education, which illustrates the correct method for educating one's children. Everyone sees intelligence precisely where it is not there. Everyone sees love right where there is no trace of it. One of the most harmful and widespread practices of Western education is to teach their children to say "thank you" when they receive something. Feel the parents say: "How do you say?" "Answer thanks to the gentleman". One of the harmful effects of this idiotic practice is that it kills in the child the possibility that he can develop in his feeling a real emotion of gratitude, gratitude. Killed this possibility through the practice of repeating "thank you" like an automaton, when she is an adult, her gratitude and gratitude will be nothing but an empty outward gesture. This emotion will not feel in feeling. These silly practices of education combined with the too intellectual indoctrination typical of European culture, they neglect to the point of killing the possibility of a real development of sentiment, which remains childlike. Look at the adults, their feeling is at best at the age of 9. The kundabuffer organ has been eradicated, therefore, there is no longer any organic reason why man should live immersed in a hypnotic sleep and all the causes of his unconscious state now reside in the wrong education that is transmitted and applied from generation to generation.

The fourth meaning consists in the fact that Beelzebub is Gurdjieff himself who tells us, through his understanding and through the ancient knowledge that has survived to our day and has always been made up of various scientific and historical knowledge, some very important facts that happened in the distant past of our planet . The guardians of this ancient knowledge had also preserved the knowledge of some important events that occurred in the past of our planet and the principles of objective science. Moreover, as already underlined, the title of the overall work, that is "Of everything and everything", is another expression used to define "Objective science". Apart from the allegory present in the 3 main characters, the rest of the work is, in effect, a literal exposition of important events that occurred in the past, and unknown to historians of all ages, of history concerning some important astronomical phenomena that have involved our planet, of objective science, of psychology, of religion, and of so much else. When Gurdjieff deals with showing the analogies between man and the universe, he does it directly, without resorting to allegories of any kind, as some others imagine. When it compares the Absolute Sun to the human brain, when it compares the complex of the Second order Suns to the spinal cord, etc., it does so directly and without allegories. When it speaks of the Moon, or of the smallest fragment that makes up our second Moon, only recently discovered, and this must make us reflect on the importance that has the knowledge of Gurdjieff, he is talking about the Moon as an astronomical body and it is not absolutely an allegory to refer to the human subconscious, as some fanciful readers mistakenly believe; also because, I repeat, when he speaks of the subconscious, he does so openly, and when he speaks of astronomical bodies, he must be taken literally.

Chapter 18 - The awareness of death

Oh Saturday ... the day par excellence dedicated to the ephemeral.

Today, October 5, is not Saturday, however it is the eve of my thirty-seventh round of the Earth around the Sun. Frankly I have no interest in these sterile empty rituals that are transmitted blindly by imitation from generation to generation, and that do not contain just nothing useful and essential for man. Arrived at this thirty-seventh round of carousel, I am aware of possessing some inner riches that no one can take away from me, they belong to me deeply and are part of my very essence. All these inner riches that can not be bought in any jewelry, I owe to one and only factor that has rooted in me to the marrow over the years, and that has transformed all my inner and outer life in an irreversible way. THE' union between my ability to know how to learn and some events that have been imposed on me by fate, have contributed to create in me this factor which is the only source and source to which I owe all my objective riches. The factor I am talking about is a profound and incessant awareness of my mortality and mortality of all those around me, it is not the superficial memory that takes place every so often in the mind, as it happens to everyone to experience, but a deep feeling and without respite. Only in this way can one have a transforming action. What matters is not the amount of years of inner practice, but the quality. So it does not matter if you have been a student of this or that other teacher, even Jesus or Buddha himself, everything does not show anything, it does not mean anything. In real life, all "spiritual curricula" are very good for blessing. I do not owe anything I own to any specific technique or practice, but only to this profound awareness of the ephemeral. Paradoxically, it was this permanent consciousness of being mortal to make me truly alive. Without feeling one's mortality one is not really alive, it is not possible to be awake, but the deep terror that afflicts each person does not allow this encounter to take place. Having terror of death is equivalent to dreading life, therefore, by force of things, those who do not feel their own mortality, die long before death completes its incessant action that begins the moment we are born. Life and death are the exact same thing, if you avoid one, you avoid the other too. It is no coincidence that the two taboo par excellence in our society is sex and death. People sleep or are already dead, and in this state they imagine a condition of happiness can exist without unhappiness not immediately following. Imagine being able to divide what in the universe is indivisible.

Life / Death, Happiness / Unhappiness, are inseparable, the moment you take one, you also took the other. For this reason, to consciously desire happiness means to desire unhappiness unconsciously. It would be like asking to have the day without the night. This is to wish for the impossible. One who is truly alive has a profound awareness that death is not something that happens a distant day, there, in the future, but that it acts perpetually, moment by moment, instant by instant. The man who lives in the past and in the future, "lives" of a dead, non-existent life, and therefore can not feel his own mortality, which is here, right now. Death is already here, now, and it has always been since that first breath that marked our entry into the world, at that precise moment, death began his work. We are all condemned to death. From this perspective, many things that occupy a considerable importance in the life of men, appear meaningless, devoid of any real value. The incessant pursuit of the ephemeral, the perpetual striving for what has no consistency, the constant childish desires of wanting to realize at all costs the sand castle that will be swept away by the waves of the sea, the vanity, that illusory claim to be something important. What's the point of all this worrying about people trying to find new penalties? It seems foolish, yet a sense has it. People prefer much more to have useless suffering, rather than face that inner emptiness, characteristic of those who have not built anything in their own inner world. People have become used to suffering needlessly, and this is no longer a problem, but the void has terror. Give him the most atrocious suffering of this world, but never the void, the emptiness. This is because emptiness, night, darkness and loneliness are all sisters of death. But there is not only the terror of the death of the physical body. There is another kind of death that terrifies people. A man whose identity is defined only through perpetual identifications with his fictitious "I" of the personality, is terrified of being awakened. For this type of man, being awakened is tantamount to losing their fictitious identities, and in this way would be forced to deal with the truth. The truth in this case is that he does not exist. A man stripped of his fictitious identity, the source of numerous illusions, he would have to deal with his deep inner emptiness, he would find himself in the presence of an abyss, and he is very likely to go crazy. Generally, we evaluate a man from his external riches, we usually ask what social position he occupies. We envy the men who have achieved economic empires in the outer world. This is because we ignore that everything constructed in the outer world is subjected to the immutable laws of dissolution. You envy all those people who have an economic empire, a certain prestige in society, because you have no eyes to scrutinize in their inner world. But the man who has no eyes to look at his inner world, will have no eyes to see the inner world of others. Being able to look into the inner world of these "celebrities", of these " and for them there is no longer any hope. The few survivors of this joyful inner global suicide, will be able to understand that the general situation can be represented through an image, that it would be good to impress in memory and not forget anymore.

This image shows a very large boat sinking slowly and on which we are all seated. This boat, however, sinks little by little, begins to sink the bow, and so we see that some die, and it is precisely those who were sitting at that point of the boat, then sinks its side, and we observe others who disappear in the nothing. But how long will we understand that we are on that boat?

The higher the peak, the deeper the deep.

Some ancient warriors said: "The spirit of man can not reach calm until he meets death."

Chapter 19 - The real starting point of inner practice

The purpose of any real practice consists in the inner liberation of man from external forces. The final goal is the achievement of inner freedom. A real inner freedom always involves man in his totality, in reason of the fact that everything within it is interdependent, therefore the liberation of only one part of it can not occur until the others are free in their turn, otherwise they will inevitably drag the relatively free part into the vortex of slavery. Generally it happens that the mind is convinced of being free but then is engulfed by the immense forces coming from the feeling and the body. Inner freedom is a consequence of the achievement of the inner unity. Based on the principle that in the universe the beginning and the end always coincide, with the only difference that they are placed at different levels, it is easy to understand that a real beginning will necessarily have to involve all the different parts that make up man in his totality. No inner practice is possible so that all the parts that make up the human being are not convinced of the necessity of this work. In general, when things are going well, one forgets work, and when things go wrong, one seeks refuge in it. This infantile and superficial attitude towards inner work leads to nothing, it is just a waste of time. As long as man can not experience his slavery with the mind, with feeling and with the body, he will never succeed in obtaining any real result. All of its parts will have to experience being slaves, and only these findings will succeed in convincing its different parts of the need to do something to obtain freedom. It usually happens that a subject is dedicated to practice before having experienced firsthand his slavery, just because he read it or heard it and believed it. Many have started to do exercises jumping this fundamental starting point and for this reason they do not get any results. The real starting point, the first fundamental step consists only in this: to prove to oneself that you are really slaves and understand what are the consequences of this slavery. Man must experience all of this in the first person, and even then he will be able to say: "I know I am a slave", until even the feeling and the body will not experience the same thing and become aware of it. If you can not live this experience of slavery on your skin, any exercise will be completely in vain, and it will only be a waste of time. To get real results, we need to start from real facts experienced in first person that will provide a direct, first hand knowledge.

Believing or not believing are the exact same thing, two perfectly useless attitudes that do not lead to anything real. If someone has skipped this fundamental starting point, they will have to start all over again. You have to be honest with yourself, and see if you have skipped this important first step, also because it goes with your life, all your life will be wasted unnecessarily without reaching anything real, it will only be imagination and fantasy. Not only will your mind have proof of being a slave, but also your feelings and your body will have to become aware of their slavery. If you have only believed what you have read or heard, everything you do will lead to nothing. If you have only experienced with your mind that you are automata that react to forces coming from outside, you will never get away with anything. All the parts that constitute you will have to become aware of this slavery, only in this way will they be able to convince themselves of the importance of inner work and not hinder each other. Finally, it is necessary to understand that the essence of this practice consists in acquiring the power of "doing" that is opposite to the state of man who automatically obeys his internal automatisms. For this reason, being humble automatically does not involve any virtue and the man who strives to be presumptuous to observe himself from another angle and fight against his automatism, even discovers that before the arrogance are never the real humble to annoy themselves but the arrogant themselves. Unconscious humility is only a mask that once removed shows the true face of the wearer and that face is the same face of arrogance. It is enough to simulate an arrogant attitude in order to verify that those who show themselves to be humiliated are annoyed, because their humility is only a mask that hides their arrogance. All this also applies to love and all other virtues. If these qualities are automatic, they are transformed in the blink of an eye in the opposite as soon as the externa conditions make the masks fall. Not surprisingly, one of Gurdjieff's rules was "Love what you do not like". Only those who love consciously can be impartial and love unconditionally, for the ordinary man the love is just a mask. Even a degenerate man like the Marquis de Sade, despite being an automaton, could see the falsity of common love, and in fact declared: "We like each other and we take ourselves. Are you bored with each other? We leave ourselves without so many ceremonies as we had taken ourselves. Will we come back to like? We recover with as much vivacity, as if we were again at the first glance. Then you leave it again, but it never breaks completely. It is true that in all this love has never entered us. But love, finally, what was it? A desire that we were pleased to exaggerate, a certain movement of the senses that the mentality of men loved to portray as a virtue. Today we know that only pleasure exists; and if one still tells oneself to love one another, one does it not so much because one believes one, but because it is the most decent way to ask oneself, reciprocally, what is needed ". However, de Sade did not possess the being to understand and all he did was nothing but a blind and sick reaction to the sexual repression of Christianity.

Chapter 20 - Attention, learning, okidanokh and the awakening of the three brains

The ability to think and feel for one's own initiative, and not as usually happens automatically through forces coming from outside, is possible only in those who, through a long and hard inner work, have managed to reach the awakening of all three brains that make up the integral psyche of man. Without having reached this state, man remains an automaton that obeys the internal automatic associations set in motion by external forces. The ability to learn and understand stops at a relatively young age and the only way to continue this process of real learning is to achieve the contemporary awakening of the three brains. If this does not happen, every illusory process of learning and understanding will only be an automatic re-shuffling of old associations from the three brains. Therefore, both the prolongation of the process of learning and understanding, and the power of thinking, feeling and acting on one's own initiative and the duration of life itself, depend on this awakening of the three brains. The states in which ordinary man lives are various degrees of hypnotic sleep, in which the link between the brains is broken. Failing these bonds, or bridges of communication between individual brains, the man works with all isolated brains. The functioning of each isolated brain is the incapacity of criticism, and therefore, it believes and obeys everything without realizing it. What is essential for getting out of the hypnotic sleep state, he is called by Gurdjieff by the name of "contemplation", a state in which a brain can observe the perceptions and manifestations of another and criticize them. This process of contemplation, of artificially generated "voluntary contacts", or of comparison between the distinct perceptions of the brains, produces a fusion of what is similar, both between the impressions received from the distinct brains, and between the similar impressions received from a brain taken individually. Then, from this degree of fusion depends what we call "degree of attention". The measurement of the highest degree of "self-remembering" to that of "loss of self" depends on this degree of attention, which in turn depends on the bonds and communication between the brains. When this synergy occurs between the three brains, they can work harmoniously for a common function without hindering each other. The principle of analogy, already highlighted in previous articles, shows us that the results of fundamental laws are manifested in all scales indifferently. Everything in the universe is alive, provided with a certain degree of intelligence and the possibility of growth and improvement. What happens in the life of the human being, also happens among all the other concentrations of the universe, the planets, the stars, the galaxies, and so on. As above, so below. The processes we have explained correspond to the second-order fundamental cosmic law that Gurdjieff calls "Ai-ei-oiua sacro". Just as it happens among the celestial bodies endowed with different degrees of intelligence, in the same way the action of a true Master, according to this law, will be to provoke a process of remorse in the pupil, working seriously on himself, he will have to criticize through the mutual observation of his brains, the old perceptions and those of the present moment. The three brains are three instruments of knowledge, and their proper functioning consists in the faculty of correcting each other. The perceptions of a brain taken singularly consist, so to speak, in 1/3 of the real world, and without the mutual participation and correction of the brains, knowledge will always be wrong. It is therefore possible to affirm that knowledge is always wrong when it is fragmented, vice versa, a knowledge is always correct when it is integral. In this sense, many examples can be made to make better the idea of the principle just stated. The very perception of the three-dimensionality of an object is due to the corrections made by one of the senses towards the other, without these corrections, we would be convinced that every object is two-dimensional, and in other cases even one-dimensional. The organ of sight perceives the objects in a two-dimensional way, but thanks to the intervention of the sense of touch, in our psyche a conception is elaborated that is closer to the truth, namely the three-dimensionality. If now this discussion leads back to the simultaneous functioning of the three centers, we will easily understand that the ordinary man lives as if he were deprived of some of his senses. Here, then, his inability to perceive the real world, which is replaced by an imaginary and imaginative perception, which does not doubt in the slightest, and indeed, defends to sword drawn. But one can not convince a blind man of the existence of light, if something can be done in this sense, it is to show him how to regain the lost sense of sight, provided he is aware that he is blind, something already extremely rare by now. Everyone is already convinced that they know, everyone is already convinced that they can understand. the existence of light, if something can be done in this sense, is to show him how to regain the lost sense of sight, provided he is aware that he is blind, something already extremely rare in itself. Everyone is already convinced that they know, everyone is already convinced that they can understand. the existence of light, if something can be done in this sense, is to show him how to regain the lost sense of sight, provided he is aware that he is blind, something already extremely rare in itself. Everyone is already convinced that they know, everyone is already convinced that they can understand.

Chapter 21 - Gurdjieff and the techniques of Mount Athos

Gurdjieff had stated several times that some knowledge had been preserved in Orthodox Christianity, while nothing useful had survived in Western Christianity. In fact, he had also declared that he had learned many good practices as they had been on Mount Athos. Not by chance, Ouspensky had found in the writings "Filocalia" certain resonances with some aspects of Gurdjieff's techniques. Also in the musical field, Thomas de Hartamann had made numerous liturgical hymns of Orthodox Christianity dictated by Gurdjieff. We find the most evident traces of these practices when Gurdjieff speaks of "voluntary contemplation" or "transformed contemplation". These terminologies disorient those who have learned the teaching of Gurdjieff through the written testimony of his pupil Ouspensky, as faithfully reported in his work "Fragments of an Unknown Teaching", as well as the book entitled "The Fourth Way", in which Ouspensky plays the role of teacher. The perplexities that arise in many people are due to the fact that in Ouspensky's works there is no trace of certain terminologies that Gurdjieff will use later in his works. One of these terminologies is, as we said, "contemplation". In the "Nunzio del bene venturo", Gurdjieff uses the term "contemplation-transformed". After that, Gurdjieff declares that the objectively higher state of consciousness stems from these third-class associations generated by "transformed contemplation". In this case, although Gurdjieff is using a "new" terminology, so to speak, the essence of his teaching remains unchanged. The contemplation of which Gurdjieff speaks, as we have already said, is nothing but the conscious work carried out on the links between the centers, as it was defined in the period in which Ouspensky was his pupil. The comparison of similar impressions that are automatically set in the various brains must now be compared and criticized through mutual observation between the centers. The centers must observe each other and correct each other. Without the establishment of ties, or bridges, between the different centers, it is not possible to obtain the observation by a center on the impressions present in another center, and on the other hand it is the same effort carried out in the reciprocal observation that favors the establishment of these bonds. The importance of this process of voluntary and mutual observation among the different centers, which Gurdjieff calls "contemplation", is explained countless times when Gurdjieff speaks of hypnotism to his students, and in the work "Views on the real world" we find it explained precisely. In the chapter "The different types of influences" in the book "Views on the Real World", taken from a lecture given by Gurdjieff on February 24, 1924 in New York, the importance of the links between the centers is explained, which allow ' mutual observation between the centers. Gurdjieff explains that consciousness, memory and critical capacity occur when one center observes another, something that almost never happens. At this point you will have understood theoretically what the "contemplation" of which Gurdjieff speaks consists, and you will also have understood that the terminologies can change, however, the essence of the practice remains unchanged. This teaching is still practiced in the epicasm of Orthodox Christianity on Mount Athos. These monks practice the same contemplation of which Gurdjieff speaks, only that they use a different technique but that has the same purpose of creating a unity among the different brains. Through the prayer of a phrase or prayer, the utmost attention is given to the meaning of each word, to such an extent that even the body itself is involved in prayer, in addition to feeling and mind. The purpose of this practice is to achieve unity between mind, feeling and body. As you can learn, then, it is the same purpose that we try to achieve through the methods of Gurdjieff that we have discussed in this chapter. If at this point, you have really grasped everything we have said, many other things will be easily clear, that is why the first rule of Gurdjieff's institute is "Do not believe anything without having personally experienced it", how they are wrong all the modern theories existing on hypnotism, of how all the ideas of ordinary psychology are fundamentally wrong, how it is perfectly useless to recite a mantra or a prayer without considering as a fundamental purpose the achievement of unity among the three brains, in order to achieve the realization of that state which is called: "All the awakened brains". In the book "Fragments of an Unknown Teaching," Gurdjieff speaks explicitly of these techniques still alive today among the monks of Mount Athos, and who were practiced in "repetition schools" in Egypt long before the birth of Christ, when Egypt it was still a lush land with no desert.

Chapter 22 - How to develop discernment against charlatans

History repeats itself and, yesterday like today, the charlatans proliferate. The main cause of this proliferation of charlatans is the absence in man of any critical spirit. The number of charlatans is remarkable, the list of these jackals who eat on the stupidity of others is immense. All the naïves asleep and quite suggestible, fall into the vortex of the cult of the personality, the opposite, therefore, of a real inner practice. Solange Claustres, a pupil very close to Gurdjieff, warned against these characters or associations that, exploiting the ideas of the master, had only commercial purposes and satisfaction of their selfishness, and led an inner pseudo-practice with harmful results for the naive researcher. Other naive, in good or bad faith, they provided indications on the common characteristics typical of charlatans, in the naive belief that this would have been useful to enable you not to fall victim to their cunning. However, in this way the essence of the whole thing is missing again. The heart of the discourse is not to believe what I am writing or what others say, but to understand how to develop discernment so that you have a personal light that will prevent you from falling into error. For this reason, the first rule in Gurdjieff's school was "do not believe anything". Now we will briefly understand the reasons for this. It is necessary to understand that experiments conducted in hypnotism have shown that when a center or brain remains isolated, it believes everything, believes whatever is said to it. The peculiarity of the isolated functioning of a brain is to believe everything that is said to it. The critical spirit is born in the moment in which a center, for example the intellectual one, observes another. When you look at all those naïve people who believe in everything and stuff the pockets of those sly charlatans so, that is proof that in them the simultaneous functioning of the centers is deactivated. Their functioning is unicerebral, there is no activity of a brain that observes and criticizes the perceptions of another brain. The attainment of discernment, of the critical spirit, takes place when the functioning of the brains is simultaneous. In this way the brains observe each other and criticize each other. From this contemporary functioning of the brains the discernment is born, the critical spirit, the conscience and the awareness. For this reason, you must understand that for you to believe or not believe, that is the proof that the three three centers are not working together, there is no connection between them, and therefore you are suggestible, you are immersed to a certain degree of hypnotic sleep. All of you will have learned that when a subject is led into a hypnotic state, it is possible to make him believe and make him do anything. This happens because the hypnotic state consists precisely in artificially provoking a disconnection between the centers. you are immersed in a certain degree of hypnotic sleep. All of you will have learned that when a subject is led into a hypnotic state, it is possible to make him believe and make him do anything. This happens because the hypnotic state consists precisely in artificially provoking a disconnection between the centers. you are immersed in a certain degree of hypnotic sleep. All of you will have learned that when a subject is led into a hypnotic state, it is possible to make him believe and make him do anything. This happens because the hypnotic state consists precisely in artificially provoking a disconnection between the centers.

Chapter 23 - The science of immortality and the secret of alchemy

Alchemy, astrology, thaumaturgy and many other systems of knowledge still lie in the realm of superstition today and are classified as pseudo-sciences. The reason lies in the fact that with the passing of the centuries the key has been lost to decipher the knowledge present in these disciplines. Originally, all these practices were based on the principles of a science that contained a knowledge of man and the universe far superior to current science. Once again the usual paradigm of considering an evolution in the field of human knowledge that proceeds from the past up to the present time is reversed. In reality, some great scholars of the Antiquities had made some exceptional discoveries that ended up in the hands of ordinary people and were misunderstood and distorted. Here, then, are the reasons that justify the reticence typical of those who possessed great knowledge. The man who wanted to learn these secrets had to be necessarily an initiate, and to do an inner work so that the degree of his being was such that he could receive and understand a certain knowledge. At a time when these great scholars of the past found themselves in the face of great wars, revolutions and geological cataclysms, they realized that the great knowledge risked to go irretrievably lost to the detriment of future generations, and so they decided that the traditional oral transmission started at first it was no longer enough. In view of this awareness, they decided to introduce the great knowledge in works of art, in dances, in literature, that just like an ark of Noah would preserve the seeds of knowledge from the deluge of human folly, well aware however that ending in the vortex of ordinary humanity it would be altered until it became unrecognizable. Through oral tradition they would continue to guard the great knowledge and its keys, while through these "arche of Noah" they would be assured of its preservation over the centuries always subject to the destructive activity of man and nature. Alchemy had to suffer the same fate when it was thrown into the circle of the uninitiated, men lacking adequate understanding to grasp their true principles. To be initially the science of the transmutation of the inner substances of man, once finished in the greedy hands of the common man who lives perpetually blinded by his selfishness, became the secret art to transform metals into gold, in other words, an instrument imaginary to get rich. The same fate suffered all the other disciplines such as astrology, thaumaturgy, and so on. Now it is easy to understand the close relationship, which I have often highlighted in this work, between the quality of knowledge and the quality of man. We have well learned the alterations that the subject of knowledge undergoes when it passes from the hands of a certain type of man to another. It has also been possible to understand that the quality of a certain knowledge depends on the inner qualities of the man who produced it. If we now remember that man is a machine specialized in the transformation of numerous and specific subjects, it will also be possible to grasp the principles on which the lost science of alchemy was founded, namely the science of immortality. The secret of alchemy consisted in the discovery that the matter called "sperm", that is the final result of the refinements that the human machine is able to perform starting from coarser materials, could be further refined to create in this way the physical body. second body in the image of the physical body, however, consisting of much thinner materials and provided with many new properties, including that of surviving death. The ancient alchemists who still possessed the real knowledge of this science, had discovered that the sperm matter could be used both to create a new body outside of itself, through union with the passive feminine principle, and for the creation of a subtle body within the same physical body, by means of special techniques of inner practice, in order to obtain immortality in this way. So this was the secret of true alchemy and of the real meaning contained in the symbolic words that summarized this process: the transmutation of base metals into gold. All the real ancient knowledge, as well as the many authentic religious and esoteric practices are nothing more than "the science of immortality", and they share the same identical purpose: the conquest of

PITAGORA

Set in his curved chair, under the vestibule of the Muse temple, recently erected by the Crotoniati, with his head decorated with a long beard, and a white hair as the linen of his garment, so Pythagoras spoke to his disciples' flower. around gathered on the day following the anniversary of his birth: "My beloved ones! This lyre of gold, yesterday suspended by you at this sacred time in memory of the day in which I was born, proves your attachment to me, and warns me of my last duties towards you. The age of rest has come to me: we are eighty; I have to say goodbye to you, and I have gathered you to do it. I flatter this sweet murmur, witness to your regrets at the idea of our separation. But in vain I would like to delay my retreat: the age with imperious voice announces that we must leave us soon, and also prevent the last blows, which envy us, and which will perhaps be the most bitter. Even from the bottom, however, of the tomb, already half open under my feet, I will watch over my friends; my soul will stay among you: and your tender remembrance, worthy reward of my labors, will prolong my existence far beyond the term to all the ordinary beings prescribed. Last night, for a premonition that I could not explain, I reviewed my eighty years. The plot of my days has not been completely regularly planned. There are too many moments of my existence, which make me blush. Io, Pythagoras, founder of a school of truth, surprised more than once not only the error, but even the lie on my lips. But since the indulgent nature gives me time to retreat, I take care to take advantage of it. Let us seek impartial impartiality not to reproach myself for faults capable of vituperating mine, and compromising your name. Two things make man, and they make him live a lot in a few moments: travel, and memory; I owe them how much I know and how much I am. Therefore, tolerate that in my last lessons, I offer you the picture of frequent and distant races, in all their circumstances and events. He spoke of it, he still speaks of it differently; and the slander, which targeted me, honored me with its persecutions. It is good, it is right that you, my friends, know me fully. Until this late hour I have believed it was for you and for me prudent not to tell you everything; still less revealed to those, with which I am only through a veil. But now is the time for nothing to be silent. At my age you have already lived, you know how to suffer or fight. So you know everything. O Holy Truth, first among the Muses, forgive, if I delayed so much to make you a homage worthy of you; but your interest itself perhaps demanded my circumspection. The splendor of your light or you fear, or you can not bear it. Few are your true lovers; and all over the world, perhaps we are the only ones gathered here in your name. The fire of Vesta burns in Rome and throughout Greece; and severe punishments await the neglected priestess, who lets her extinguish the flame. O Truth! Where are your altars, your priests? This school serves her as a sanctuary; we will be the ministers: and when we separate, everywhere with us we will bring the precious seeds. Many will lose it; but as long as they germinate at some point in the globe, our labors will not be fruitless. Perish from Pythagoras up to the name, but remain the truth. All of you, that you listen to me, be the guardians, and, if it is necessary, become martyrs. Obliatemi also, but always speak the truth: I recommend it before everything and above all. Love each other, and be truthful; I could restrict myself in these two principles: they include all the others. Abari, Zaleuco, Caronda, Timarato, Elicaone, and you, Liside, the most assiduous of my students: you, my chosen disciples, use all your means, so that the truth may become the legislator of the districts who gave you the day. You, Zamolsi, who never abandoned me, goes under the bearskin that covers you, bring the truth to the semi-barbarian inhabitants of Thrace. You, Milone, so famous for the strength of the body, whose nature he endowed you with, know that a great garrison is also the love of truth, and this will give you more luminous triumphs than those already decreed in Crotone and in Pisa. My beloved disciples, I must make you, though regretfully, a confession. As an example of Buddha, one of the legislators of India, all that I have taught you so far, resembles those eroded coins that are circulated to the lack of pure metal. But it is time that I pay your attachment to my person with the purged gold of the truth, which I have kept in reserve for these last moments. Only the lessons you are about to listen deserve to be considered: the others were nothing but preparatory to these. The instruments of music are thus tested; he is made to give them false sounds; dissonances, before arriving at agreements based on an exact calculation. You dedicated me many of your years; I want to realize all of mine: what you could have demanded by entering my school. My mistakes, my faults will not be hidden from you, because you will know how to take advantage of everything. I leave to your prudence the care to propagate the strong truths that you will hear, and to put them within reach of youth, women and the people; for the education of the two sexes and public education will be the two principal objects of our detentions, as they were of all my studies, and of all my travels. My faithful friends! When I will no longer be among you, plant distant distance signals above the earth, of the signs of truth, because you need points to reunion in political proclaims, because I am not that Encytis, son of Mercury, who obtained from his father the distinguished favor of living and dying of each other, and of preserving the memory of these two states! Although I feel like a son of Apollo, I realize more and more that man was simply born.

Fragment taken from
" Pythagoras in Egyptian and Babylonian esoteric schools"
Sylvain Maréchal - 1827, 1828.

GURDJIEFF AND THE CARE OF CANCER

Patients have a tendency often marked to believe that few of the real progress can be made in the art of healing. However, medicine, of which it is said to have been rather an art than a science, inevitably tends to become a positive science, and this thanks to the incessant applications of the new scientific methods. Advances in chemistry have allowed us to isolate the active ingredients that the ancients, in their intuitive ignorance, attributed to herbs. Organic synthesis allows us to recompose substances that are increasingly similar to those of our tissues. But one should not believe that the progress of medicine lies exclusively in chemistry. Living beings undergo, at all levels, the action of physical agents and chemical affinities represent only a small part of these agents. It is the time when we attribute in physics a preponderance place to electricity and radio-electricity, and we pretend to explain all the matter through the electron and all the movements through the waves, it is indispensable not to disregard the power of these important agents in therapy. A worthy French scientist, that the fate of humanity does not leave indifferent, Mr. Georges Lakhovsky, has precisely undertaken to fight these student gaps, in light of the works of his illustrious predecessor, Professor d'Arsonval, in which it is measured that natural and artificial electric waves affect our existence and that these forces can be used to maintain our health and for the treatment of our diseases. The oscillating circuit method devised by Lakhovsky, whose application is already so fruitful, is the result of a long series of research, as well as of so much theory and practice, on the origin of life and the problems for the treatment of cancer. This great innovation is dealt with extensively in his works: "The origin of life", "The universe", "Contribution to the etiology of cancer", "The secret of life", where radio waves are no longer considered only the perfect medium of our communications, but the very principle on which the universe rests, in particular organized beings and life. Mr. Lakhovsky's observations, findings and experiences imposed on him the inescapable necessity of explaining the phenomena of biology through the electromagnetic waves, in particular the secrets of instinct. He has come to show, in effect, that only the waves are capable of guiding the animals over great distances, so as to allow them to communicate with each other and the outside world. It is in this way that Mr. Lakhovsky conceived the oscillatory nature of the living cell and organized beings, in the same way that physicists have conceived the oscillatory nature of the material molecules, of the atom and of the whole universe. This hypothesis is progressively verified through his experiments so original and so fertile on the treatment of cancer and other diseases. It is easy to understand why the living cell is a small oscillator and electric resonator. The cell is in fact constituted by a nucleus immersed in a liquid, the protoplasm, surrounded by a membrane. Now, the core is essentially composed of tubular filaments of insulating material containing inwardly a saline conductive liquid of electricity. These filaments, so twisted on themselves inside the cell, are therefore real small oscillating circuits, in all respects identical to the circuits, coils and windings of the receivers. The living cell can then play the role of an emitter and receiver of short-wave radio waves, which determine very high-frequency electric currents in its nucleus. Now the vibration of an oscillating circuit is maintained by the radiant energy and we can ask where the energy that makes the animal and plant cells vibrate, which together forms what we call "life on the surface of the Earth" . After a few years, astrophysicists have revealed the existence of natural electric waves of various wavelengths and in particular of very penetrating waves, which due to their universal nature, have been called cosmic waves. These waves, which come from the interference of all the radiations of the stars, they have such a penetrating force that they can cross a seven-meter-long slab of lead and fifty meters deep into the ground of a certain constitution. It is also very probable that certain cosmic waves exist that can cross the whole Earth. Mr. Lakhovsky has succeeded in demonstrating, through numerous experiments, that the cellular oscillation of living organisms is sustained by cosmic radiation. However, a drawback results from the constant variation in the intensity of the field of these waves and their frequencies, and therefore in the rotation of the Earth in the cosmic universe. The extreme variation of these waves explains precisely the difficulty of maintaining the cellular balance of living organisms, and therefore their health. It is allowed to believe that, if the cosmic waves remain constant in value and frequency, we would not contract either illness, suffering or death. The problem of maintaining health therefore returns to the constant maintenance of the vital oscillation and, therefore, in the regulation of the field of cosmic waves around the subject. Such a concept seems to present a great novelty, for those who have not been accustomed to medicine for a long time, to stand above the point of view of chemistry and to bring biological actions back to affinities. But, at the same time, chemists are forced to resort to electricity to explain their reactions. The notion of cellular oscillation, which Mr. Lakhovsky has so clearly defined, is no longer singular, on closer inspection, than that of the microbe. Thus, in his latest work "The secret of life",

" What is a microbe? Is it a microscopic animal with mouth and teeth to devour the healthy cells of the surrounding tissues? Nothing like that. Does it act by chemical reaction as if it were a corrosive substance? Not at all, since it has a composition almost analogous to the cells to which it is attached. The microbe is simply an oscillating circuit, which by means of a coupling with the healthy cells, forces them to oscillate on a different frequency from the one that characterizes them, or to better stifle their oscillation by introducing electric resistances into the circuits of these cells (toxins), and also emits a parasitic radiation that suppresses by interference the typical radiation of healthy cells".

The disease, a struggle between the microbe and the healthy cell, is therefore due to an oscillatory disequilibrium caused by the alteration of the cellular vibration that is under the action of the microbe. In general, and the same for those suffering from microbial disease, the disease results from an oscillatory imbalance due to the weakening or excess of cellular radiation. Thanks to his investigations in all branches of the physical sciences, Mr. Lakhovsky has come to show that there are permanent natural causes of oscillatory imbalance, such as those deriving from the nature of the terrain. A reinforcement of cosmic waves is produced in conducting soils of electricity, such as plastic clays, marls, ferruginous soils and carboniferous soils. These radiations and the resulting interference, they favor a rapid division of healthy cells into neoplastic cells, such as to form cancerous tumors, or well causing the oscillatory disequilibrium of the cells that thus generate diseases. To avoid the negative effects of the oscillatory imbalance, it is essential to ensure, by means of electrical filtration, the regularization of the cosmic field that surrounds the living organism, as Mr. Lakhovsky explained in detail in his work called "Contribution to the etiology of cancer". These results are obtained, acting on the electrical constants of the cell and modifying its chemical composition, surrounding the subject with many oscillating circuits having the function of electric filters. Here is how Mr. Lakhovsky explains the operation of this filtration: "We know that the terrestrial atmosphere is the site of a considerable quantity of electromagnetic oscillations of all wavelengths and of all intensities, therefore of constant and innumerable electrical discharges (lightning, etc.). On the other hand, we know that all the electric collector and brush motors, all the magnets, all the traction, power rectifier and the most varied electrical applications, create a large field of permanent auxiliary waves in the atmosphere. . In addition, for about fifteen years, the Earth has been covered with a very tight network of factories that produce radio waves, radiotelegraphy, radiotelephony, etc., which is currently impossible to find a small free and available place in the range of these waves. In these conditions, it is conceivable that it does not matter which oscillating circuit, the dimensions and the shape that is capable of producing, in this vast field, the proper waves on which it is possible to oscillate; It has therefore been found that it is necessary to use an oscillator that generates local waves, such as the cellular radio oscillator, with which Mr. Lakhovsky healed the geraniums inoculated with cancer in 1924. "

Here is the logical and rational explanation of the oscillating circuit used by Mr. Lakhovsky, who in the second series of his experiences was able to heal the geraniums inoculated by cancer. In fact, under the action of this constant field of the pulsed radio waves in the atmosphere and resonating them, the oscillating circuits create a local field, which channels and filters in some way the cosmic waves necessary for cellular oscillation. This filtration is however a general phenomenon. It has been found, in fact, that rays such as light, ultraviolet rays and other electromagnetic radiations, radios, X-rays, etc., do not have properties, according to Mr. Lakhovsky, that to act the cosmic waves both in advantage that at the disadvantage of cells. In reverse, the fields created by means of the lakhovsky oscillating circuits, bring into play a very lightly maintained force. They always act in such a way as to facilitate and facilitate the oscillation of the cell, and by filtration of cosmic waves, regulates cell division in a regular and permanent manner, and this explains the vigor thus produced in the cells, which allows them to fight victoriously against all diseases and against all microbes. After the first treatments on geraniums, of which we have spoken, and which were the object of communication between the Academy of Sciences and the Society of Biology, the methods foreseen and recommended by Mr. Lakhovsky, have been successfully applied in hospitals clinics on numerous patients, under the indication of their doctors, both in France and in foreign countries. The scientists, after having long familiarized themselves with the medical applications of electricity and radiation (radiotherapy, radiology, ultraviolet rays), they have thus begun to understand the importance of the discovery of Mr. Georges Lakhovsky, and wanted to offer him support to put into practice his methods and experiment with oscillatory therapy. Not only in France, but also abroad, they accepted the theory of cellular oscillation with extreme interest and did not delay to apply the treatments recommended by Mr. Lakhovsky. Professor Attilio Sordello, cancerologist, director of the radiology service at the hospital of Santo Spirito in Rome, obtained through these methods the results so positive, that he did not hesitate in May 1928, to present a detailed and precise report to the Congress of Radiology of Florence. The reader will realize, thanks to the observations we have collected in this book, that the diseases have been successfully treated through the Lakhovsky method, which consists in the application of one or more oscillating circuits in the form of bracelets, necklaces and belts. . Other remarkable results have been obtained in the numerous cases of cancer, even those in a very advanced state. We generally come to localize the evil, to suppress suffering, to cause the regression of the disease, and to produce a marked improvement in the general state of the body and even a rejuvenation of the organism. Mr. Lakhovsky wanted to communicate a certain number of observations among the thousands that have been successful,

Adapted from
The electromagnetic waves that heal: from Nikola Tesla to Georges Lakovsky
EMB Presta

THEORY OF MESMERISM
by Prof. Taddeo Dei Consoni, 1849.

All the Magnetizers, who took care to write up to this day, attributed to the magnetic effects two distinct causes: the fluid and the will.

They attributed the greatest strength to the will, and demanded that it have a positive action on the patient subject, subjected to the action of Magnetism. It is to this will, that they assigned the first efficacy of the relative phenomena (which they sometimes translate with words of intention or thought,

Mr. Lafontaine, is quite contrary to this opinion adopted by the Heads of the School of Mesmer doctrine.

He is convinced that there is only one and only cause, a whole physical cause, that is: the nerve fluid, that is the vital fluid. This invisible cause like air, heat, electricity and gas; impalpable like light, it was called Magnetic Fluid; subsequently, Animal Magnetism, by his Theory, does not seem to me to be the same as telling us, in what constitutes its quintessence; therefore I believe it will not be bad to my reader, if in other words in this note, from beautiful principle to better define and then explain that it is Animal Magnetism, that is what you think obedient, This place, I will say, seem to be able to call, and better to understand Animal Magnetism: the influence that animals exert on each other, both by touching themselves and by acting at some distance, when they mutually change their respective way of existing, by effect of the nerve fluid, which is slendered by the magnetizer, or communicated by its contact and insinuated in the nerves of the patient, capable of even investing inert bodies, vegetabili and minerals in addition to animals perhaps of any order. This fluid, which is what Jussieu means by Electro-Calorific, Faria calls Epoptism, and that I would say to be the vigil of the soul during the death of the body, since I call sleep the death of the body (at least in appearance), is a very powerful agent, both because he governs and governs the functions of the human organism, and because he is capable of making him suffer the greatest alterations. In order to better designate the Animal Magnetism in the Sleepers, it would first be necessary to know what the Soul is and to be able to define it well: and that is why I feel, not to formalize, if in procuring to say what really is this fluid, I can not make up for that with some circumlocution, which however seems to me to be adequate to give an adequate idea: much more, if you want to compare these expressions with the words of other writers, who for want to define the anthropopo-magnetism and the zoomagnelismo, that mounts what was here meant by Animal Magnetism, said: to be the action that man can exercise on his like, on himself, on the vegetabili and on the minerals. Others said: to be the manifestation of the faculty, which naturally possesses all beings to act upon one another, and each one on their own organization; these definitions are too universal, and worse than that of Plato on drowsiness. But we must not be surprised at all this, because St. Jerome himself, talking about Magnetic Sleep and Sleepwalking, he called them sleeps. This fluid was now generally called Animal Magnetism in honor of F. Anton Mesmer, who if he was not the inventor first, was at least those, who first exposed the theory that concerns him, which attracted and conciliated the attention of the Sapientl of all Nations at least in modern times. He was born in Weilor near Steiu on the Rhine in 1734. Mesmer devoted himself to the Medici studies and was a pupil of the famous Van Swieten and Haèn, obtaining the Doctoral degree in Vienna in 1766. He appeared later in the scientific world with an inaugural thesis, in which he poured around the influence of the planets on human bodies. He made his first experiments in Paris, and wanted to prove, that the celestial bodies exert a direct action on the nervous system of the animals, through a very thin fluid, which penetrates them from all sides. He intended to be able to determine this action through the very general properties of matter and organized bodies, such as gravity, cohesion, elasticity, irritability, and electricity; and the more his theory developed, he meant: that as the alternatives of gravity produce the phenomenon of the ebb and flow of the sea; in a similar way there are different perodic returns also in animal bodies. This susceptibility of the animal bodies to be continually under the influence of (celestial) bodies and of the earth itself, seems to have been what it intended to call Animal Magnetism, and which others called the vital, circulatory and modifying principle of all human beings, through flow, reflux and currents.

Although the Magnetism is called Animal, for the reason already mentioned, we should not intend to be its influence only on animals, because as I just said, it still invests the vegetable and even mineral bodies, which can be called, in some way, organized; but it is also called animal because it is a fluid that flows along the nerves of the animals, but can invest organisms of any nature, but only because they can be the agents exclusively animals, and more properly those who have pronounced the ganglia and related organs, for communicate it or to prove its power. With the expression advanced then, that we are continually under the influence of the celestial bodies, I do not intend to refer the absolute concept of Mesmer, but only the expression and at least a mere idea of him, although it seems to be possible to believe that it was part of the doctrine of Toaldo also around the influence of the moon to be a satellite of the earth. yet again I argued perhaps invincible arguments, proving the great influence of the moon on earth bodies, corroborated by the result of long observations and experiments, but the place to reproduce is not appropriate here. It would seem better to be able to call Universal Fluid, for the reason, which is found everywhere, and which animates everything. Thus, the hypothesis of Ippocrates, who taught to be an inner, occult, universal principle, would be the closest to the truth. proving the great influence of the moon on earth bodies, corroborated by the result of long observations and experiments, but the place to reproduce is not appropriate here. It would seem better to be able to call Universal Fluid, for the reason, which is found everywhere, and which animates everything. Thus, the hypothesis of Ippocrates, who taught to be an inner, occult, universal principle, would be the closest to the truth. proving the great influence of the moon on earth bodies, corroborated by the result of long observations and experiments, but the place to reproduce is not appropriate here. It would seem better to be able to call Universal Fluid, for the reason, which is found everywhere, and which animates everything. Thus, the hypothesis of Ippocrates, who taught to be an inner, occult, universal principle, would be the closest to the truth. When heat, light, electricity and other fluids, which are modifications of the same principle, develop when the bodies contact, their friction, their affinity, such as:

1: in the inner membrane of the larynx, the trachea, the bronchi and the interstices of the lungs for the air that penetrates continuously anc gives its oxygen to the black blood, from which it resumes its life and its heat after having given it to the bodies where it returns;

2: in the membrane of the pharynx, the esophagus, the stomach etc.: for air, food, drinks;

3: in the endosmosis, or intracapillary electricity, etc., this heat, this electricity, these impregnable fluids so developed, are transmitted to the nervous apparatus, and from there to the brain, which through innervation transmits it to the whole fabric; and to have a test, by passing an electric current along the main nerve of a member separated from the body, the contraction of all the muscle fibers of this member is determined, which receive the filaments from this same nerve.

Man can not therefore live, that with the continuous development of caloric, electricity and other occult and mysterious fluids, which result from the movement of its parts and molecules, and from the chemical affinities that operate in it. A famous Physiologist says that the caloric, the modified electric fluid, like any other imponderable agent, maintain life in the same way, as in putting into action the contractility in the nervous substance and in the fluid mollecules, which are in contact with them. This is what we can doubt. It seems that above this primitive theater of life, the phenomena of affinity occur, the transformations of the fluid proper to the nervous substance, as happens in the blood that flows through it to nourish it and to give it in means of action.

Dutrochet made experiences, from which it results, that there is an intercapillary electricity in the living bodies, to which we must attribute the movements of the fluids in the bodies. The contact of liquids electrifies solids, the organic sensitivity of living solids; and this property of receiving electricity is the agent of organic and vegetative life.

It is the universal fluid announced by Mesmer, and suspected by Newton, which is disengaged under the name of the most subtle spirit, which penetrates through all the solid bodies hidden in their substance. It is the fluid that presides over all the acts of life, the mysterious ohenomena of the attraction of the sexes and of reproduction. No doubt that the medicines do not act, if not for the same principle, with which the minerals act, which are decomposed, and which are formed under its influence, in the same way that the vegetabili do, which grow quickly under the his current, and the animals escape his action.

Since all the Wise men now recognized that man has a very particular atmosphere, which has its principle in the universal fluid, modified by our organism; so now for us, no more evidence is needed for the existence of the nervous or vital fluid.

Under the empire of the will, it seems that a function similar to that which occurs in the lungs on the inspired air works in the brain, and that the universal fluid experiencing a change loses some of its properties in order to acquire other essentially vital ones. nervous system before being issued. The brain, the spinal cord and the nerves, which are distributed throughout the body, are innafliati in all their parts by an abundant arterial blood, which produces the vital fluid, while the organs are the depositaries and the conductors. It is the vital or nervous fluid, essentially necessary for life, that one needs to communicate to a foreign body, to produce the phenomena known under the name of Animal Magnetism.

The ends of the nerves reach the outer surfaces of the muscles, both inside and out, at one or the other. At the surface they terminate by means of the arranged organs, in order to receive, and to transmit conventionally to the nervous center, the action of the external bodies. It is with the help of this very particular System, that under the empire of the will, we can transmit the nervous fluid. The nerves serve us as conductors, and then transmit it to the patient, who receives it communicates to the nerve center.

I would like the will to be the concentration of intellectual ideas over a single idea. It acts on the principal nervous center of the Magnetizer, above all on the brain, and causes the emission of the vital fluid in more or less quantity; it communicates it to the patient's nervous system, astoundes it, and develops the effects, which are generally observed in magnetized persons. the magnetic phenomena are therefore the consequences of the invasion of the nervous system of the Magnetized by the vital fluid of the Magnetizer. The cause is unique, physical and material: it is the vital fluid.

The will we have, acts only in us, producing a more active secretion to the brain and contractions to the plexuses. For this reason a greater quantity of fluid and intensity in the action is caused. The more this will is expressed with resolution, the same emission is overwhelming and intense. We can therefore reasonably assume that magnetic phenomena have a single and unique cause, which is the nervous or vital fluid, and that the will is nothing else in this case, than an accessory, as in all other things. What he did think, that the Will acted on the subject, is one of the effects that arise in the state of Sleepiness. A sleepman who has come to a state of lucidity, sees the thought of the Magnetizer, and obeys the mental order given to him by him. This is not, that a transmission of ideas; for this reason it was therefore concluded that the will, to which the subject was subjected, was to be the cause, but this is an error. The cause was confused with the effect. The transmission of ideas is one of the effects dependent on the particular state in which the patient is located. The will can not act physically on another body, because it is within us and accompanies all the acts of our existence. We do acts of will by raising the foot, holding out our hand, and on all occasions in the end, this will manifest itself, when its own influence seems to abandon our idea. But with the sole will, we could not magnetize anyone, if we did not find ourselves in a state of health and convenient strength. If we are tired, or weakened by stale physical constitution whatsoever, we will not produce any effect or very little, notwithstanding that we apply ourselves with a great will; whereas, on the contrary, if we are robust and healthy, without any will, magnetizing mechanically and with distraction, we will produce in spite of positive effects. It is not already believed that the result of the Magnetic power depends on the strength of the muscles. To be a powerful Magnetizer, one must be endowed with a happy physical constitution, to which they can not make up, neither the vigor of the body nor the insistence of character. We have observed men of herculean forms, of all vigor and firmness, not producing any magnetic effect; when, on the other hand, there were people, whose physical strength seemed nothing, but who had a very sensitive and highly developed nervous system, to obtain almost ready effects.

35781113R00187

Made in the USA
Middletown, DE
08 February 2019